Pr

MW00964694

Meditation has helped me personally to have inner peace, joy, love for myself and others. It has opened me up to experience better physical health and psychological stability. The Vedantic concepts of meditation, dispassion and kriya have been so beautifully described in this book by Dr. Vasudev that I am sure every reader will wish to learn more and consider such wonderful techniques as part of their daily routine.

—Florence Green, RN

This masterful creation is not only revolutionary in its purpose; it's like Holy water on dry desert land. Dr. Akshya Vasudev opens his heart and shares his sacred Self throughout these pages. This is a rare read indeed. As someone that has experienced psychiatric services personally and professionally, I found Akshya's message beyond refreshing! My own sacred Self yelped in glee repeatedly while I had to resist the temptation to tell the world. It was a profound honour to receive emails with, "for your eyes only", in the subject line while Akshya polished the final manuscript. My eyes experienced the privilege of reading Divine Wisdom making Its way into words as I drank it all up like a parched prisoner. If your sacred Self has felt imprisoned and dormant and is now ready to receive this book; the Truth contained will help free the wellspring of wisdom within you. It even has the potential to awaken psychiatry by putting 'soul' back into 'psyche' and making recovery an epidemic versus relapse. A radical paradigm shift in psychiatric services is being called for more than ever. It's time to address mental distress with a biopsychosociospiritual approach and put an end to the incessant hamster wheel. We are spiritual beings having a human experience. Is it any wonder we experience an imbalance when we forget to nurture the human Spirit?

—Rev. Laurie Nevin, Ordained Spiritual Counsellor

This is no ordinary spiritual book. This is not a typical spiritual book. This could be the book you have been waiting for. This is a book of Love. The first time I read Dr. Akshya Vasudev's masterpiece, Be YourSelf, before I was halfway through, I was overcome with joy and felt immediately compelled to find him at his place of employment so I could embrace him in a hug full of Gratitude and Love. Alas, his assistant informed me that he was helping a client. Not a surprise. I didn't have the time to wait but I wasn't disappointed because I knew on a spirit level he was already feeling my Love for his gift. If you are a seeker on the spiritual path to enlightenment, this is a must read. Akshya has channeled the message of the Divine with skill and grace. The words fall gently into your heart and the heart thanks them with the knowing that they have found their home. Be YourSelf is not a hard read like some spiritual books full of complicated ideas and concepts. You will recognize the content as if it was written for you, by you. Thank you Akshya from the bottom of my heart for a treasure that is sure to transform lives across the Universe and I humbly thank The Divine for Dr. Akshya Vasudev.

—**Jeff Nevin, Fellow Spiritual Seeker with Lived Experience**

The typical physician and typical seeker believe that medicine and spirituality are mutually exclusive. Conversely, self-development is the most efficient, the most effective aid to our physical and mental wellbeing. I have known Akshya for many years and he is a unique physician-seeker trying to integrate these fields. This work is a loving, insightful, practical expression of every being's potential.

—**Acharya Vivek, Chinmaya Mission Niagara Falls**

Be YourSelf

Spiritual Awakening for Everyone

Dear Letiüa & Mian

Be YourSelf.

Akshya

Dr. Akshya Vasudev

◆ FriesenPress

Suite 300 - 990 Fort St
Victoria, BC, V8V 3K2
Canada

www.friesenpress.com

Dialogue between King Vikram and Karkati permitted to quote from the book
"Vasistha's Yoga", ISBN 9780791413647, published by SUNY and authored by
Swami Venkatesananda
Confirmation by
Sharla Clute
SUNY Press

ISBN
978-1-4602-8734-7 (Hardcover)
978-1-4602-8735-4 (Paperback)
978-1-4602-8736-1 (eBook)

1. SELF-HELP, MOTIVATIONAL & INSPIRATIONAL

Distributed to the trade by The Ingram Book Company

Table of Contents

This is _____'s personal inspiration page.
(Insert your name here)

I will live with the faith that I am close to the Divine at every moment of my life. I have the faith. On this journey I will come across days where doubts will occur. Doubts are transient and help me strengthen my faith even further. I will regularly reflect, contemplate, and meditate to take away all doubts.

I know my Self because it is there, everywhere, all the time. So let me be ever calm in this faith.

I will aspire to learn from every situation because I have been born to evolve into a higher state. Each moment that I am living is special and I am alive because I am special. I am living in this Divine world created by Him.

I will always have a smile on my face. When I smile the world smiles back at me. That is the natural thing human beings do. If I feel in despair, I will smile back at my moodiness and my smile will return. I will then smile outwardly for people to enjoy my smile and they will be happy too. I will always remember that my smile is a reflection of my true nature, which is calm and serene.

I will take the path of the virtuous. Virtuosity is Divinity. However, I will not find fault in the person who lacks virtue. He is ignorant and has not found his Self just yet. I will embrace the person who lacks virtue. He needs more of my compassion rather than less. I will find the Divinity in everything and everyone. This whole creation, made by Him, is blessed. I will help uplift everyone that I come across with a gentle smile and my warmth.

I will work, wherever there is an opportunity, not for the salary or the praise, but because work is Divine.

I will not seek happiness. Happiness, sadness, worry, rumination, obsession, and paranoia are only emotions, and by their nature they will present themselves to me. I will examine each emotion, observe it from a distance, and not be affected by it. These emotions are a product of my mind, which by nature is fickle. I am more than my mind. My inner nature is the Self, which is immeasurable joy and calm. This Self lights up each and every person around me as well as this creation. I am that Self. I am omnipotent – omnipresent. I am the Divine.

Acknowledgements

I DEDICATE THIS BOOK FOREMOST TO MY MOTHER; SHE IS THE reason that I am here in this world; to my departed dad for instilling the values of self-discipline and seeking the truth; to my brother for being ever dependable and loving; to my wife for being my strength and for her generous nature in being tolerant of my idiosyncrasies; and to my two daughters who have been a source of unadulterated and unconditional love.

This book would not have been possible without the guiding light, knowledge, instruction, and intuition provided by my teacher and guru, His Holiness Sri Sri Ravi Shankar. I pledge to continue to read and to listen to his knowledge so that my ignorance recedes.

My guru's words have been published and are in common domain for everyone to read. I have applied my own interpretation to some of those published works in this book. I wish to additionally acknowledge other sources of knowledge which I have read and have helped shape some of the thoughts expressed in this book including Vasistha's Yoga, Commentary on Ashtavakra Gita by Sri Sri Ravi Shankar, The Gospel of Sri Ramakrishna, Commentary on the Bhagavad Gita by Swami Chinmayananda, Autobiography of a Yogi, the Foundation and Advanced Vedanta Course by the Chinmaya International Foundation and countless discussions with Acharya Vivek. Expressed in this book are my own interpretations and I acknowledge that these may differ substantially from the commentaries by Men of Perfection. As a seeker I remain in the process of learning.

I thank all the spiritually awakened souls who are in close proximity as well as those who are on social media, who motivated me to initiate and complete this work.

The Self is limitless. Any words of acknowledgment, if they were to be offered to it, would be like offering the rays of the sun back to the sun. Hence, I salute the Self.

Foreword

DO YOU SOMETIMES FEEL WORRIED, TO A POINT WHERE IT HURTS? Have you suffered from pangs of moodiness when you just can't seem to get out of your blues? Do you sometimes feel that you are lonely and that nobody cares? Do you have no energy and wonder why you are alive? Do you sometimes obsess about the way you look or have thoughts about being dirty? Do you sometimes feel that people are looking at you and talking about you and you just don't understand why you have such experiences? Do you sometimes feel the pangs of guilt when you have had one drink too many and the next day your body feels the hangover and you curse yourself, "Why did I succumb to my desires to have more than I needed?" Do you feel immobilized with fear and dread of the past because of some trauma that you suffered? If you answer yes to any of the above, this book is for you. If not, then it still might help you understand why a loved one goes through such symptoms.

If you believe that there is a spiritual reason for these symptoms and you are open to helping yourself, then this book is for you.

If you are curious about why you were born, or why you were born into the family that you have, then this book is for you.

If, on the other hand, you feel that spirituality is of no value to humanity and only materialistic things are important to help us move forward, then I would like to thank you for your interest too. Perhaps you might find this book an enriching experience if you approach it with an open mind.

CHAPTER 1. The Basics of Spirituality and the Science Around Mental Health

IF YOU ARE READING THIS PAGE, THEN THAT MEANS THAT YOU ARE really interested in knowing more about your true nature, your Self. You have a desire building in you, perhaps a realization that you are much more than what you see. You are more than your body, your feelings (mind), or your thoughts (intellect). You are open to the idea that the concept of human consciousness, intuition, and virtuosity is as important now in the modern scientific world as it was thousands of years ago. You are curious to investigate and know how you and this whole creation work and exist. You want to know and explore the reason why you were born. You wish to use a scientific enquiry lens and are open to knowing and accepting new ways of understanding how our body, mind, and intellect work. So let us begin this chapter with some questions and answers, as if we are conversing with a person of Wisdom.

Can I be a human being without any distress or feelings of despair that life is moving too fast and I just can't find the time to get off this merry-go-round? Why do I have some days when I am swathed in feelings of unhappiness? Why do I sometimes feel so irritated at work, despondent at home, and restless at night? Why can't I let go of that vague feeling of tightness in my stomach I get at times? Why do I feel so

upset for no obvious reason, as if my mind has taken over
me? Will I ever be able to just relax and let me be me?

Yes, you can live without any stress or mental health issues. Let us call such a state enlightenment. This state of being is within your grasp. It is up to you when you wish to be enlightened. The choice is entirely yours. You just have to grab the opportunity available to you right now.

Enlightenment is not an elusive concept reserved only for the learned sages. It is an option waiting for everyone like you and me. Just drop your inhibitions and preconceived ideas and you will find peace in your Self; the everlasting peace and quietude.

You might be born or inculcated into a belief system or a particular religious faith. It does not matter. What matters is that you are a seeker who is looking for answers, which some people call the truth. Finding the truth is a process; it is a journey – a journey with a beautiful beginning and a path that is self-revealing when we have the right intention. Intention is all you need. The rest will happen.

All the prophets of the past, be they Jesus, Muhammad, the sages of Vedanta (Hinduism), Confucius, or others, have provided us with wonderful, beautifully written books of knowledge and they all boil down to very basic messages of wisdom. Whatever your belief system, religious background, or understanding of spirituality, across all of these messages the knowledge seems to be the same. The Divine is present everywhere and you are a part of this creation. The Soul or Self in you is the same, and it is present in everything and everyone. This Self is limitless in its potential. Just keep this knowledge as the centre point in your journey and let the magic begin.

You did not answer me at all. Don't make me more confused.
Is there a God? What are God and the Soul? Why am I here
on this planet? What is the purpose of life? Is there life on
other planets? Can I be enlightened?

Wonderful questions. Keep the spirit of inquiry open. Only with a scientific bent to your questioning will you be able to get the answers.

These above questions do, though, reflect the dichotomy between science and spirituality, which most people **think** that we should have. However, even the brightest of the bright and the best scientists have recognized that not all answers can come from science alone. It is spirituality that can provide all the answers. In fact, spirituality is nothing but a science.

As you become more spiritually awakened you will start to find the answers yourself. Just remain calm in this knowledge. The seeker gets as much information as he wishes to find. As he grows spiritually he loses all his fears, neither fearing the guilt of errors from the past nor suffering apprehensions about the future. He even loses the fear of death. He becomes resolute and successful in his actions and yet is quiet from inside.

People may have understandable worries about embarking on a spiritual journey. Preconceived ideas in someone who is a spiritual seeker might include: that he becomes too innocent and gullible, unable to live effectively in this materialistic world; that he will face lots of obstacles; and that he will have to live in misery or poverty. There is no basis for such thoughts or beliefs. The person on the path of spirituality becomes more innocent in heart, child-like, and yet is super-intelligent. Innocence and intelligence go hand in hand for such an awakened person. He becomes fearless. He strikes when he has to, just like Prince Arjuna, who got enlightened through his instruction from Lord Krishna. Arjuna then became instrumental in winning the epic battle, *Mahabharata* (the great battle of Bharat, India).

The enlightened person's understanding of why we are alive and what makes people think the way that they do, is much clearer than that of the person who is not enlightened. He appreciates the goodness in everyone yet understands people's motives more fully. He is able to sense what other people are thinking so much better. He starts developing intuition about what is going to happen. His heart is full of compassion, yet he is more resolute in his decisions. He is not shaken by bad news nor does he get exuberant and grandiose by good news. He is wise and knows what is best for him, his family, and society. He never gets agitated. He lives the life of a majestic lion, knowing that in this world there is nothing to fear. All "obstacles" are considered as mere toys in the path; he loves to play with them rather than being affected by them. He moves forward steadfastly without any fear of failure and does not show jubilation over success. Material wealth may come into his path, yet he is not affected by the value that people place on money and comfort.

So don't fear the spiritual path, just embrace it.

Another fear might be that someone who has endured suffering cannot be enlightened. The truth is otherwise. In the depth of misery is a spark, waiting to be stoked and cherished. Spirituality provides the knowledge to grow, to forge a path, and to attain enlightenment. The person who has endured pain has let the body, mind, and intellect become ready to be chiselled into something ecstatically beautiful.

Enlightenment is a stage where all of your questions turn into wonder. The journey to enlightenment begins from inwards. Stop looking outwards for your answers – you will find them through constant reflection and contemplation. You don't even need a book to find the answers. All that is needed is an open mind and the sensitivity to accept what is true. The answers are in your Self – all you have to do is to grab them.

A word of caution though, an enlightened person does not go around telling all the answers to everyone and the person who claims to have all the answers is not enlightened yet! Yours is a personal and special journey. Remain unfaltering and resolute on your path.

The process of enlightenment is similar to that of the gentle opening of a rose; from a bud to the splendour and radiance of a full-blown flower. It takes time, but is without effort, and the results are obvious to everyone, including you.

We all can be enlightened; we only need to have faith in this concept to get on the path and remain on it. If you feel that you cannot and will not be enlightened, then indeed your wish will be fulfilled. But the very fact that you have so many questions is a predictor of your enlightenment.

Let us begin our inward journey by first looking outwards. The very existence of creation is a proof of the possibility of enlightenment. Just open your mind and observe. If you were to examine each aspect of creation, be it a bird singing, water flowing down the river, the sun shining bright, or the day and night cycle – all of it is so beautiful that it is a bit unreal and magical. The magic pervades each and every aspect of creation, every inch, every atom. Perhaps one of the main reasons that we are alive is to just revel in the knowledge that everything that the Creator has made is special and we all have special roles. With this wonderful understanding and acceptance, every moment of your life becomes a celebration and you offer each moment in gratitude to the Creator. You can let any state of mind like worry, apprehension, sadness, despair, obsession, paranoia, and addiction, just fall away in these feelings of celebration and gratitude. There is no choice for these feelings but to dissipate. Just have the faith.

Take a pledge to yourself that you will henceforth try to live in the present moment in gratitude and hence you will have no reason to get tainted by expectations of the future or guilt about the past...that you will live in the present moment, centred, alive, and with joy.

The learned ones mention that all aspects of creation are connected. We are as much connected with our parents through a blood relationship as we are connected to the pesky neighbour, the boss who just does not seem to listen, the secretary who never gets the work done the way we want her to, as well as the politician who seems to give so many promises that are never fulfilled. On a good day we feel that we are connected with good people, on other days we feel connected to even the not-so-good person. Whatever is the emotion or energy that drives this connectedness, is so difficult to describe. Perhaps this connectedness shall provide a clue as to why we are here.

It seems that there is a sort of a force or an energy that connects us to others as well as to the insentient things. So what is this energy? This energy might be responsible for all that we can see and are trying to understand more and more by using modern science. Isn't it interesting that we are now able to see the far- away galaxies using increasingly bigger and better telescopes AND we can see more and more of smaller things through gene-based techniques and the electron hadron collider, which are allowing us to manipulate the code, so to speak, of why we are living. Science continues to go deeper and deeper into seeing and trying to understand the basic building blocks of life. However, enlightened masters through the ages have told us that we ourselves ARE and we BELONG to these macroscopic and microscopic levels of our reality. And perhaps to more that we cannot yet see.

Let us call this force or energy Divinity, or the Self. Various religious and faith practices call it by different names. You can perhaps identify with that name. But for the sake of this book we are just going to use the words the Divine or the Self as that keeps it simple and we all like simplicity.

If there is Divinity in everything that we see and that we cannot see, what has that got to do with me? Why am I here on this planet now? Why are there good days and bad days? Why do I feel so crappy on some days while on others I feel, yeah, life is good?

Have you noticed that we actually feel a bit empty and sad when we have just finished enjoying something that we thought was good? Can you recall the blankness that you experience after having a big meal, after an orgasm, or after having seen the latest blockbuster? Why does that good feeling not last? Perhaps we are trying to find that feeling of goodness IN something that is transient. That lovely pie that we ate was just that; a bit of food that stimulated our taste buds, made our satiety centres excited, and released a bit of dopamine and endorphins in the right places in the brain. Then those levels returned to normal and we suddenly had a bit of a let-down feeling. Perhaps that is the reason we don't want kids to have too much sugar as they become "too high" on the sugar rush. Yet, we do want to enjoy the next succulent piece of meat or delve into the wonderful taste of a warm, cheesy pizza. It now becomes clearer to us that it is our sense organs, be it the tongue (food), touch (sex), eyes (looking beautiful in front of the mirror), smell (food!) and hearing (pleasant words) that seem to have control over our minds. So, as a seeker, the right question to ask is: Where did these five perceptions come from in the first place? Is there an energy or Divinity that allows us to breathe and live and therefore have these perceptions? Think.

> *Hmm. That is interesting. So that means that all these sense organs work due to this primeval energy of some sort and I am enjoying it. So what is wrong with that? By your defini-tion, the Divine made these things and these sense organs for enjoying creation. So then why do I feel unhappy and listless after I enjoy these sensations?*

The answer is very simple; these organs of sensation are provided to us as a window to appreciate this world. The problem starts to grow when a human being becomes completely stuck in the enjoyment of the sensations. His desires grow and he forgets the source that provided these sensations in the first place. If the person gets stuck on getting his desires fulfilled, he forgets the bigger picture. He becomes agitated without even realizing it, and other people see him as irritable or upset. As you reflect and contemplate, you will realize that it is the grip that these desires have on you that makes you feel listless. Just let go of your "need" and the desires will stop troubling you.

> *So are you implying that if I am to be a seeker of Divinity, I have to stop enjoying these things, which the Divine has provided me to enjoy? Do I need to be a recluse and stop enjoying life? Well then, I will definitely be sad, won't I?*

No, the answer is in a few practices: reading knowledge daily so as to gain wisdom of our true nature, self-discipline, and meditation. They are complementary and essential. The intellect needs self-discipline so that it can keep the thoughts and feelings in check. Self-discipline is a way of life that is the easiest to initiate but also the hardest to follow through on. Have you not noticed that the people who have made it to the top in whatever that they do tend to be very self-disciplined? If we want to make our lives better, let us bring positive change through self-discipline. You will see that people who maintain a daily routine appear more relaxed and calm than those who ditch a routine at every pretence. The person who reflects and contemplates before going to sleep, sleeps at the same time every night, and gets up fresh and refreshed, has a wholesome and productive day. The mind, being fickle by nature, will want to entice you to enjoy that late-night party, to spend more time on Facebook and Twitter, to watch too much on the idiot box, to have the additional drink that you don't need, or to eat one more morsel of food. These sensory perceptions of our minds titillate us. But we are more than the mind. We are also the intellect and our souls. The intellect tells us, albeit sometimes as a small voice in our heads, not to overindulge ourselves. And when we have over-indulged, then perhaps we feel a bit of guilt. The guilt smoulders because we have not let it go, and then it will breed agitation, depression, and anxiety. We yearn for peace but don't know how to get it. So let us not be dependent on our sense organs and the momentary pleasure that we get from them. Let us continue to look inwards for everlasting peace.

If we were more self-disciplined; not yielding to every indulgence that we come across, our minds will be less taxed, our intellects will be at more ease, and we will feel more relaxed. Simple. We can try self-disciplining our bodies by practicing daily routines and good dietary habits. Slowly, over a period of time, self-discipline will make our intellects sharpen and not bend in to our minds and sense organs. Note that I am not advocating for a special diet or for you to stop enjoying the things that the Divine has provided to you. Restraining our sense organs makes our minds even more agitated. The trick lies in keeping to the middle path. Don't under-do it or over-do it. That is the trick. Discipline yourself so that you can enjoy life more meaningfully.

Consider scheduling a regular time to read words of wisdom from the learned, to speak with people who have read this knowledge, to think and reflect on this knowledge yourself, and lastly, to meditate. The knowledge that we gain by reading a scriptural work can be truly beautiful if we come to it with an intense interest in knowing. The wisdom that we gain touches our innermost desire to be calm.

For any seeker, meditation is the quintessential way of knowing our own Selves, learning to let go of our expectations of the future and our worries about the past. Meditation is a state and not an act. Constantly meditate on your Self, your true nature, and you will never get agitated. Meditation does not take time – rather, time becomes available to you as you start practicing meditation. As you meditate regularly, slowly the sense organs' control over you starts to recede, your lower vices start falling away, and you become naturally relaxed and peaceful.

Gautama Buddha's mindfulness is a form of meditation, which more and more people are learning, while others are researching other forms of meditation and breathing techniques. Research shows that these techniques are excellent treatment options for a number of physical and mental health conditions. One of the most important teachings of Buddha was that we should all remain in the present moment. Do enjoy the piece of cake – enjoy the flavour, the texture with every morsel that you put in your mouth. However, do not compare it with that other cake that you ate from that other shop. Then you are going into the past. Rather, feel grateful that you have been given an opportunity to live your life and enjoy the cake. The more grateful we are, the more beautiful the world seems. Do not let your sense organs decide your life. Instead, let your intellect grow stronger so you can appreciate that these sensations are only transient and there is likely a deeper source of joy and energy, which provides the life-giving form to these sensations.

We dictate our state of happiness, not anybody else. We also hear about people feeling "stressed" at work and at home. Others might suggest to you that some amount of stress is inevitable and needed, so that we can meet our deadlines and work adequately. Sadly, they are wrong. Remember that stress is just a state of mind; it is artificial and we do not have to live in stress to perform adequately in this life. Rather, gratefulness for every sensation that we perceive, for every opportunity of being alive, for every breath that we take, will help us become more joyful and able to do the same work with ease and a smile. This might sound difficult to achieve initially, but as we open our minds through gratefulness and meditation, we reduce our extraneous interests and we start feeling the warmth in our souls. We learn to become happy all the time.

Your inner nature is calmness and serenity. You can and you will be able to take this path to enlightenment.

How can I live in the present moment when all the time I am bombarded by emails and media informing me about the next famine or hurricane or corruption, and by people gossiping and blaming others?

Stop blaming your family members, your friends, your work colleagues, your enemies, or world politics for your unhappiness. If happiness is a state of mind, then you are much more than your mind. Revel in the knowledge that you have a much bigger potential. You just have to recall that your nature is of complete and eternal bliss. Remember that when you were a just-born child you only cried when you needed attention. Otherwise you were so calm and relaxed. Over a period of time we just forgot to remain joyful and contented. Even now as adults don't we love to goo-goo and gaa-gaa with a toddler? When we are with the unadulterated Divine presenting through the innocent eyes of a young child with no hint of an ego, we abandon our own stiffness and become close to our own Selves. Children bring out the Divine in us!

We, as human beings, love to find happiness. But our biggest problem is...let us use the word "ignorance," as it is the opposite of "enlighten-ment." In our ignorance we continue to try to find happiness in others or outside of ourselves. The only reason two people might find that they can't live together is because they **think and feel** that they have differences. It is usually their egos speaking, when one person is trying to prove a point. Have we not seen this in our day-to-day lives? We feel hurt the worst when our most-loved ones point out our mistakes. Our egos are so big that we feel they are doing this on purpose, that there is a nefarious reason for their actions. These egos are only a small portion of us, but we have allowed them to grow so bold and strong that they seem to occupy centre-stage in our lives without us even recognizing it. The ego is nothing but our ignorance of our true nature.

Let us learn how to remove ignorance through Vedanta. The differences that we see in people around us, be it in terms of shapes, sizes, colour, or personality styles, are what make each of us special. The biggest antidote to the ego is the knowledge that the Divine made everything around us. So how can we even think that there is no Divinity in people with whom we are annoyed? Perhaps the only reason we are upset at them is because they have just pressed on our sensitive points, which are based on our previous experiences. And we, as human beings, are so fragile in our hearts that we feel easily pressed upon. The fact is that the person who is annoying us is projecting those bad feelings in us. This is such a common process and so ingrained in us that we do not even consciously recognize that it is happening. Growing up from children to adults we have been barraged by peer pressure to conform in a certain way that society demands of us. We are constantly trying to compare our behaviour with that of those we think are evil or not right. But we don't need to judge. All we need to do is acknowledge, with our ever-sharp intellect, that we continue to find Divinity in everything and everyone. It can be done. Lots of people have done it. They don't mention about their secret. You too can be a seeker or a yogi and keep it quietly to yourself. Just have the faith. Keep this knowledge a secret in you and try to keep company with people who always have smiles on their faces, just like you.

But how can I keep this faith that you talk about? There are so many faith-based religions and spiritual techniques. Which one shall I take up? How will I know that I am on the path?

They say faith in the Divine grows by two ways. First, when we are really down in the dumps, when nothing seems to be going right, when we have lost a loved one, or when the job that we have wanted for such a long time does not seem to come to us. And then something happens. We remember somewhere in our minds that perhaps there is a Divine energy; God, Allah, Jesus, Holy Spirit, *Bhagvan,* and so on and so forth. We yearn for an answer from the depth of our despair – to be relieved of the pain. Our faith then grows and the Divine shows us the way. Have faith that everyone finds his or her faith, it is all but a matter of time. Of course, some people have to wait a bit longer than others to get this revelation. Just let go of any doubt that you might have and embrace the power of the Self and you will instantly be pulled out of your ignorance.

Another way our faith can grow is when we are just grateful for what we have. Every opportunity to breathe, to communicate, to live life is offered back to the Divine as gratitude. The Divine rewards in subtle ways and our faith keeps growing. Both ways bring us closer to the Divine.

These are the only two ways. If you feel that you are losing faith in humanity, Divinity, and in being alive, the only reason for it is that you have started to question this faith because you think that He has not shown you the path just yet. But that is what faith is about. If the principle of developing faith is so simple, all we need to do is let go of our preconceived ideas and start either being grateful or to acknowledge that within the depth of misery we will find faith. Do not question the Divine. The whole world that you see around you is because of Him. You are only a small part of the world.

Here is a secret to propel your faith in the Divine. When you are really having a bad day, just ask yourself, "Why am I feeling like this?" Take a moment to pause and focus your concentration on your breathing. Feel each breath going in and out. Concentrate on your breath and let go of your stress. You will notice that the emotion of feeling bad just passes within a few seconds.

Another way of letting go of your stress is to just go out and look up at the sky. Then you will realize the non-significance of you. You are such a small entity compared to the entire creation. It will likely be humbling and help you get rooted to the spiritual path. Try it out.

I will tell you another secret. Get a pet, especially if you have never had one. Perhaps you are an extrovert, and you have lots of people to give you company with whom you feel at ease. Or you could be an introvert and enjoy more of your own company. Loneliness and isolation can affect either of these two personality types. Such physical states breed feelings of depression and anxiety. Getting a pet can help. It not only provides you a companion and helps you to get some exercise and practice self-discipline, it also helps you to appreciate the Divine in little things.

Another secret. There can be more lasting feelings of joy in our day-to-day affairs. Isn't it interesting that feelings of bliss can come when we have tears in our eyes? Remember the scenes in the movie *Titanic* that brought you to tears. We feel much more joyful when we see an act of compassion on the screen. The Coca-Cola advertisement in which someone is doing something positive for someone makes us feel joyous. So compassion is perhaps the most joyful virtue. Hence, lots of people want to volunteer their time. But here is a secret within the secret. You can show compassion, find the joy, and even get paid in the process. Volunteering does not simply mean that you are doing something and not getting paid for it. It is the intention rather than the act itself that makes you feel joyful. Giving with the right intention is where joy lives.

Sometimes people say that compassion seems to suck out the energy from you. That belief is also not true. Compassion begins from the heart, as we call it, but it is actually the Self. And our Selves are limitless. Each of us is connected to the eternal Self. If He created everything, then will he let the Self in one person be selectively depleted? That does not even sound logical.

Now this is getting very interesting. So how do I recharge my batteries after I have shown a bout of compassion?

Well, goodness and joy come back to you, if not instantly, at least in a short while. That is a given. The quickest way to recharge is by meditating on the Divine who will make you feel complete in a few minutes. Guaranteed.

So to summarise, here are the facts: Give with the intention to help someone and you will instantly become joyful. Secondly, meditate regularly. Nobody and nothing will be able to take your joy away from you. That is it.

To really stay on the path of spirituality, you do need a guru or a master. Someone who is a seeker needs to have someone he can look up and listen to. As per Vedanta, the ancient text from which Hinduism as a religion has developed; the word guru stands for someone who takes us from ignorance and darkness into the brightness of enlightenment.

If you have not found your guru yet, don't fret, you will soon find your spiritual teacher. A bigger secret is that when you are ready, your guru will find you. It could be anyone. Some people who have become enlightened have even found gurus in things around our world such as the sun, the water, and the air. Each of these elements gives so much and asks for nothing in return. Again faith comes into play. When you find your guru, things will change and everything will look magical. Just hold his hand and he will lead you. He will not let you fall.

CHAPTER 2. My Past

LET ME START WITH A STORY. EVERYBODY LOVES STORIES. I WILL start with my own.

I grew up in a well-provided-for Hindu family with no strong religious affiliations. My father would eventually retire as a high-ranking officer in the Indian Army while Mom, besides being a homemaker, also taught mathematics to high school students.

Growing up as the older sibling, I certainly had the privilege of receiving new things first. I got the first bicycle, the first *Tintin* and *Asterix* comic books, new clothes, and new toys. My brother was likely envious and we frequently fought. Yet, the memories from my childhood are more of love than dispute. It was an unsaid love, which did not have to be expressed. It just was.

Other memories of childhood are rich and colourful. I remember living in a small, one-bedroom house in Agartala, the capital of Tripura, one of the eastern- most states of India. Dad modified the place so that the front porch was converted into two bedrooms; one for each of us brothers.

Dad was innovative and playful; that is what I remember most about his nature. These qualities were likely due to the culture of the Indian

Army. The army certainly encouraged them in its officers, as well as in their children.

I recall being at home, spending time with my parents, enjoying time in the back yard with my younger brother, hiking in the forests with my dad, playing with touch-me-not plants, listening to the squawks of our pet ducks, and running and fooling around with my first dog, Bobby. At a young age I understood the value of respecting our parents. Dad's position as the senior officer in the small community of an artillery regiment was evident to all of us in the family. He was the commanding officer and with this came a lot of responsibilities. Inevitably he was off on the firing range, or far away from home engaged in war games.

I must have been seven years old at that time while my brother was five. I recall being with him one late afternoon, exploring Dad's offices. We were not supposed to be there, but the excitement of doing something different was too enticing. We stumbled into one of his unit's war games rooms. It was an amazing room! Everything was so captivating with wood models of tanks and jeeps, and artillery guns in different colours. The dust in the room was bouncing around in the late-day sun, making the place look even more magical. But soon the shadows became longer and bigger. Our hearts started to race and we felt scared. We looked at each other and then both ran away from the room. Neither of us would accept that we were scared! Our young egos were indeed blossoming then.

I had my first touch with a difficult situation a few months later. One early morning before going off to school, I was out on the lawn with my dog, Bobby. And then I saw a shadow of something, or perhaps even someone, hanging from a litchi tree just beside our house. It felt ominous; whatever it was looked too long and dark to be up on a tree. It was certainly not a bunch of litchis. I wished to investigate but Bobby's incessant barking stopped me from getting closer the tree. I felt scared and ran into the house. I remember I had tears in my eyes and I hid my face in my mom's nightgown. I can't remember what she might have said, but I know I was asked to get ready to go to school immediately. Mom also got ready to teach at the same local Catholic school where I was a student. I can't recall talking much that morning.

I do, though, remember feeling confused and scared the whole day. I just could not concentrate in class. I really loved my English teacher, but that day nothing seemed to be of interest. I don't recall Mom making a special effort to come and meet me later for lunch, but then memory is a strange thing. You can only remember certain things. When I got back home, our *sahayak* (helper), an enlisted soldier, whom we would fondly call *bahaiya* or brother, told me that the shadow I had spotted that morning was the body of an enlisted soldier who had likely taken his own life. I was told that this person had been having some marital issues. It was likely that this person had snuck out of his quarters in the middle of the night, to hang himself.

Everything about the incident was hush-hush from then on. There was no culture in the Indian Army that permitted talking openly about such a difficult situation. I was too scared to ask my dad while Mom seemed a bit aloof, if not indifferent, about the subject. So I must have learnt that suicide should not be talked about.

Time moved on. I remember Dad being a self-respecting man. He always had a smiling face, which suited his tall, thin, and lanky stature. He would organize the loveliest picnics for the other officers and their families. It seemed that if he was not on the firing range, he was organizing one picnic after another in the remote hills or gardens around Agartala.

The town was quiet and close to the border with Bangladesh, a country that had been liberated from Pakistan just a few years before. I remember going to the local market every Sunday with my parents. Mom loved to shop and Dad would always oblige. "Smuggled" goods from Western countries, routed from Bangladesh, were openly on sale. The Indian economy was still in the throes of pseudo-socialism then. There were hardly any Indian electronics or high-quality textiles available in many parts of the country. Hence, even though we were living in a small town so remote from the rest of India, it was considered a good posting, at least from my mom's point of view, as she had an opportunity to buy much sought-after Western items.

Dad's pay was a pittance back then. I remember he had to regularly send money to his parents to support them and his three sisters. Once a year in the post, he would always get his rakhi from each of his sisters. It was a beautifully decorated garland that he wore on his right wrist. He took the act of tying a rakhi, a very traditional Hindu expression of love and solidarity, very seriously. It was a faith established through a simple piece of thread on the wrist.

He had three sisters and wherever he was posted in India, he would still receive his rakhis through the ever-reliable Army Postal Service. I, however, had no sister, so Mom would tie me a rakhi too, and I would wear it proudly the whole day.

We did not follow many religious practices at home. In fact, it was a bit ironical that though I was from a Hindu family, I went to Catholic schools for most of my school years. Mom and Dad must have had more faith in the Catholic education system. Certainly the reputation of army schools was not the best, and Dad's postings were often in places where good schools were difficult to come by. During my early years I felt no pressure to change my religion from the Christian nuns, but I really loved the hymns and prayers in the morning assembly. The very humble "Our Father, who art in Heaven....give us this day our daily bread....lead us not into temptation.....for ever and ever" was the loveliest and I would raise my voice louder every time we chanted it in assembly.

Dad loved music, especially English pop, as well as disco and dance music. Sometimes he would put on hymns and *bhajans* (Indian devotional songs), which I could not make much sense of. On Sunday afternoons, he frequently made us go with him to the unit temple, where we would listen to a lot of bhajans sung by enlisted men's wives and the priest or *Pandit ji.* (Any person who has reached a position of respect gets a suffix of "ji" in Hindi.) I used to frequently feel in awe and stare in wonderment at Pandit ji singing those bhajans. The music felt so charming and peaceful. I can't recall Dad participating much beyond lip-syncing. None of the other officers either actually took the microphone to sing any bhajans. Even to my young eyes it was obvious that it was the enlisted men and their wives who sang, while the officers and families would participate, albeit superficially.

Soon after the temple services, the officers and their families would take off to their high teas and evening parties.

No one really talked about God or spirituality at home. However, I was very interested to find out more about things that I did not understand. I started to read whatever spiritual material I could lay my hands on. Bible stories came first as they were taught to us in school. I was very shy then and would hardly ask any questions. I kept to myself. After all, how could I ask spiritual questions when Mom would sometimes cry when Dad was away and all the responsibilities of running the house fell on her shoulders? It sometimes felt that I had to be there for her more than Dad could be.

Soon the whole unit got posted to the western part of the country, to a much larger cantonment called Nasirabad, near Ajmer, Rajasthan. It was more than 3000 kilometres away. Everybody in the unit was excited. Our journey would be on a "special train" and everyone would be travelling together. All our luggage, pets, and toys, would go along with us on the train. All the officers were in first class, non-air-conditioned coaches, with four people in each cabin, while the enlisted men were in the regular, second-class coaches. We started off in the hills of Assam and slowly made our way through the jungles of the eastern states, down the gorgeous valleys created by the River Ganges. I recollect exotic food being served at all railway stations, days of not being able to take a bath, waiting for hours to pull into a large railway junction, impromptu singing and games by the officers and the men, and laughter and merriment. Wonderful memories. What I most cherish of these potpourris of memories is just the poking of my head out of the train wagon door and feeling the fresh air on my face. It felt so heavenly. Of course that feeling would get spoiled whenever we would pass a brewery or go through a big city. I really did not enjoy the smell of big cities even then.

Mom helped us make our house a home in Nasirabad. It felt as if we had been transported from a tropical Eden to a palace in the desert. Our house had previously belonged to the commanding officer of one of the old British Army units. The house was huge, with more than twenty-five rooms in the main building and at least an equal number of supporting rooms for the sahayaks. We even had a bath in each of the five bathrooms! We had never seen anything like that. So far, we had been used to taking a bath with water stored in plastic buckets in a small bathroom. Now we had an option of choosing a bathroom just to take a wash. Now that is called opulence and luxury – to come back from a hot day and just sit in the cool water in the bath.

Life settled reasonably quickly in Nasirabad. My brother and I started to attend a Catholic school in Ajmer. My strongest visual memory of that school is being slapped hard on the back of my hand with a leather belt by the principal because I was late. It felt cruel as it was not even my fault. The army bus, which transported us, was delayed in arriving to school that day. Everyone from our bus faced the same treatment.

If the Father, who was a school principal and whom we looked up to, could punish us for not being wrong, then what sort of values did he wish us to learn? I lost a bit of faith in Catholic rules and started to hate Christianity and its values. I kept my thoughts to myself and did not speak much about this to anyone.

My anger erupted on a different day. We were returning from school on the army bus. A boy much larger than my brother was teasing and beating him. I would usually never become involved in such situations, as I knew that my brother could fend for himself. He was small in size but knew how to handle himself. But that day I just lost it. I took off my belt and banged its big metal buckle onto the boy's head. There was some bleeding and the driver of the bus went to the nearest Army hospital clinic so the boy's head could be stitched up. We were late getting home that day. I faced a few words of reprimand from my father. But somehow I felt relieved about what I had done. In psychiatric parlance, I had shown displacement. I displaced my pent-up anger onto someone else. Interestingly, I have never had to hit anyone else in my life. Somehow, something had just snapped in me that day.

A few years later we moved to the big and bustling city called New Delhi. I loved being able to see so many new things in the big city, but I didn't like my school or the four houses that we had to live in. Each of the houses was small compared to our home in Nasirablad. With our bahaiya, Mom looked after us as Dad got posted to Jaffna, Sri Lanka, fighting the Tamil Tigers, and then to another city, Allahabad in the state of Uttar Pradesh, whilst we stayed behind in Delhi moving from one house to another.

My school in New Delhi was known for its rowdy kids, but I still found a few friends that I could associate with. I was moving into puberty and strange things were happening to my body and me. I was constantly embarrassed by my pimples and wanted to hide away. I became very conscious of my looks, felt nervous talking to the girls, and became even shyer. The only refuge that I could find was in my curricular books, PG Wodehouse novels, Hollywood movies, pop music, occasional cricket, badminton, and swimming.

I hated the city, as I could not be outdoors frequently enough to enjoy nature anymore. I could not disappear into the woods as I had in Agartala or go on long walks in the neighbourhood in Nasirabad. I remember, though, if I had enough of reading my schoolbooks, or had a bad day, I would just take my bicycle out for a long ride on the reasonably empty roads of Delhi Cantonment.

Whenever Dad returned home on his annual leaves we would go out on hikes and picnics with him. We went deep into the forests in the centre of the city, called The Ridge. There we spent hours walking and practicing shooting our air-gun. I became a good marksman as I could hit tins of empty food boxes kept more than 150 yards away. I remember hitting some crows and pigeons successfully, but I didn't enjoy that at all. On a subsequent posting, of Dad's to Guwahati, one of the largest cities of Assam, his fellow officers invited me on a hunt. We were using a shotgun. I must have been twenty years old. I remember feeling very uncomfortable with the proposition of actually killing an animal on purpose. I intentionally aimed really badly that day and did not have one "successful" shot. Nobody noticed my poor aim. Little did they know that I was actually a very good marksman on the shooting range.

I started to work very hard at school and eventually would be at the top of my class in high school, but I remained very shy. Talking to any girl, especially if she was good-looking, would bring me into a sweat. I remember one day I got laughed at by a gorgeous girl in my class. I had only been able to muster just enough courage to ask her if she would be attending a particular dance party at the Officers Institute. I must have been sixteen at the time. I just could not make myself ask her out to the dance. I was in so much fear and apprehension that my whole heart seemed as if it would come out of my chest. I vividly remember her giggling as if she was mocking me. After that, I hid deeper in my protective cocoon of curricular activities and did not go out on any further dates in high school.

Mom was by then getting increasingly dissatisfied with life in New Delhi. To make ends meet she started to teach mathematics in a high school. She complained bitterly of the long hours wasted on school buses. I also think she missed the parties that she was used to in Nasirabad and Agartala. She also used to complain about relatives in Delhi and their greed, how big the city was, and how much time it would take us to visit them. She grumbled that these relatives just did not seem to be of any help when Dad was away, but only called us if they needed things from the army canteen. The canteen was a supermarket with prices at least thirty percent cheaper than the local market.

I recognized how lonely she must have felt with Dad being away a lot. However, I remained pleasantly happy in my books and in my own loneliness. My brother and his male friends were great company and did take away the boredom at times. I dabbled a bit in learning the guitar but would never have the courage to perform in front of an audience. I remember wanting to make an impression with the girls and I did take my guitar with me a summer camp where I performed a couple of pretty good songs. However, when I tried to join a particular song being led by one of the girls that I'd taken fancy to, my hands froze and I just could not strum the guitar even though I knew the notes. I kept looking into the ground, scared shitless. I hoped I could disappear into thin air.

The best part of camp was going on the magnificent hikes in the jungles and mountains in the Himalayas. The snow-capped peaks, the coohs of the mynahs, the ice-cold water from the brooks, and the wonderful light and warmth from the daily campfires enthralled and captivated. It was just heavenly. By this time I had learnt that the most peace that I could find was when I was close to nature.

I wanted to read more and subsequently broadened my repertoire to science fiction, crime, nature discovery books, and cheap thrillers. I even started to read a bit of Christianity again.

I was now getting to be a young man and there was some amount of pressure to find a vocation. It had become quite obvious to me at this stage of my life that the world revolved around certain rules: You needed a job to make ends meet. The job should lead to some sort of reputation and position in society. Your position in society helped you get married and then you became "settled" enough to enjoy your life. A respectable job brings enough greenbacks to keep the machinery of a household going. I had to think of a job in either medicine or engineering as they paid well, so the quality of life would be good.

I followed these rules and I studied hard for the last couple of years in school. I got into one of the best medical colleges in India and thought that life would flow easily from there.

How wrong I was.

I just could not find myself in the top of the class any more. Now I was competing with the best of the best. If I had been a nerd in my class in high school, now I was competing with super nerds who could memorise all the arteries, veins, and nerves of the dissected hand within a matter of a few minutes, while I would struggle to learn it in a day. People were cramming all the time using various abbreviations and acronyms.

I hated it. The spirit of inquiry, careful observation, making deductions, and coming to a logical and reasoned conclusion were all gone.

Perhaps my exasperation and lack of confidence stemmed from my experience on the first day of medical college. It was something I had not expected. I had been warned that "ragging" was common but did not realize how vicious and demeaning it could be. However, it was all supposed to be for "fun" and to make us "stronger." Well, coming home late at night even though college finished at 4:00 p.m., and seeing the worried look on my mom's face, did not help. She asked a lot of questions as to why I was late and I could only meekly reply that everyone was being ragged and so was I. That was it. I simply didn't have the courage to give any more details. I felt extremely uncomfortable about letting Mom know that I had to play sexually provocative scenes as part of an impromptu skit in a public park; I had to learn new, sexually abusive words; to sing out loud from the top of the school building; to hurl the choicest abuses on everyone on the street; to sit in the position of a male hen for a period of time; and so on and so forth. My mom would have been devastated that her eldest son was facing such humiliation after she had made all that effort to protect me through my younger years.

Dad got posted out of Delhi to Guwahati in my second year at medical college. I had to stay in the college hostel. Thankfully there was no more ragging. Rather, I tried to gel into my role as a second-year student. I now had to subject the freshers to ragging. However, I just could not make myself rag another student. It felt grossly wrong. I was thankful that nobody noticed that I was just a mute spectator.

Life carried on.

Hostel life was so different from the protected environment of home. From having my own room in my childhood to having to spend all of my leisure and study time with two other men that I did not know well, was not easy. Thankfully one of my mates turned out to be one of the nicest guys that I have ever known, while the other one used the room mostly to leave his stuff while he would sleep with various women in and out of college. So it was not bad at all. Unfortunately, the food was horrid in the college cafeteria. There was only one flavour of food served – no flavour. I desperately missed home food and the spices that I was used to. Inevitably we ate out every day. Dad sent me around sixty dollars every month and that was more than enough to put gas in my scooter, watch a few movies, eat out, and pay the college and mess bills.

Life did change, mostly for the good, in my extra-curricular life. I started to speak the college language, and felt more comfortable in speaking it even though it was full of filth. I spent time playing various sports. I dedicated myself to getting up early in the morning to do my studies. I continued to make an effort to go to sleep by ten p.m. most nights, so that I could get up by five a.m. Some of my friends made fun of my nocturnal habits but they knew I would not budge from my schedule except to watch a late-night movie once a week, or during the annual college cultural festival.

During that time, I started to have pangs of anxiety and mood swings for no obvious reason. I remained quiet about it though. Nobody talked about such stuff. One person from my college year took his own life and nobody seemed to care. There was no enquiry or debriefing. It was *a part and parcel of life – suck it up – keep living – forget about it – it does not matter – he had it coming*, were all the unspoken messages. There were frequent nights when I had difficulty in going off to sleep. I started to use a sedative, an over-the-counter pill, in the hope to get some sleep, but it made me feel rotten. I tried to swig a couple of shots of dark rum on really bad days and that would make me sleep for a few hours at least. But the next day I would feel crappy and I couldn't keep my eyes open in class or concentrate.

So I just stuck to sleeping less. My grades suffered and I scored just average in my grades. This was one of the really down times in my life, indeed a trying time with no support groups and no guidance available from peers. I had not found my guru yet nor a soul-mate. For the next couple of years, I continued to stay a bit aloof and distant from others.

However, kinship grew with a group of eight batch-mates, who came from similar backgrounds with either Catholic, public-school, or army backgrounds. We mostly spoke in English, enjoyed rock and roll, had similar tastes in food, shared similar jokes, and had a vision to change things for the better for the world.

Lofty ideals started to appear in our heads. We wished to make a difference. We particularly got upset about a particular Supreme Court report called the "Mandal Commission," which led to the requirement for all professional colleges to have fifty percent of their seats reserved for people from Scheduled Castes, Scheduled Tribes, and Other Backward Classes. This was not what Mahatma Gandhi would have wanted! He had promoted steps to make sure that the caste system would be scrapped. His vision was that this had to be done at the grass roots level; at the levels of schools where education was supposed to be equal. It did not make sense that somebody who had scored far below average in high school should be made to compete with intellectually bright students in a medical college. I don't know if these thoughts were politically correct, but those were our views at that time. We protested and went on processions around the hospital as well as outside of it. The school's dean, I guess, had no option but to call in the police when things did not settle after more than five days of ongoing processions called *dharnas*. We were taken away for a few hours to the local jail to help us cool down. Everybody knew that if we had a police record we would never be able to get a job anywhere in the country. We kept quiet for those few hours and by late evening when we were released from the jail we were as quiet as rats!

In my last few years of medical college I started to date a bit and my shyness slowly began to disappear. Perhaps maturity was finally settling in; likely it was self-confidence after having been with the brats at the college hostel.

By the final year of medical school I realized how many youth were in the same boat as me. Life was no longer about grades. We started to become a bit serious regarding our potential jobs as doctors. I found many role models in some of my professors as well as seeing so many others that I would never like to resemble. I started to love seeing patients. However, internal medicine was not for me – too much of remembering details about each and every disease and different diagnoses based on remembering blood levels and markers. Yuck! Perhaps surgery would be more appropriate; my professor made it appear so easy. He was so good in what he did – everything was effortless. All his patients seemed to respect him. He was always on time for rounds, precise in his approach to planning a surgical procedure, inclusive of everyone on the team, gave information to patients in very simple language, and most of all did not seem to have any ego.

A few weeks into my surgical rotation in the fourth year of medical college I developed acute pain in my abdomen. I suspected it had something to do with the chronic diarrhoea that I had endured over the last four years. I just could not escape the poor quality of drinking water in the college mess as well as from roadside food vendors in the city. It was likely that I had an appendicular abscess. The pain was excruciating in my lower abdomen. I got myself seen by a senior registrar in surgery that evening and he confirmed the diagnosis and suggested that it was best to get operated on that very night. But I protested and refused. I was so confident in my professor that I wished to be seen by him and him alone. I had to wait till the next morning for his assessment. And he was there for me. His compassion and professionalism were obvious throughout his consultation. He cared and I was put on the elective operation theatre list. He took exceptional care of me while I was being wheeled into the OT, as well as post-operatively and during follow -up. Now that is the type of doctor I needed to be!

I knew my mother would have liked to be there for me during the surgery but she was more than 3000 kilometres away in Guwahati. I don't know what must have gone through her mind as she worried about her son. She was used to calling me at seven a.m. every day since I had left home.

The day of the surgery dawned and a ward orderly shaved me around my private parts very skilfully. I felt embarrassed but the guy was a professional. He did not even once look up to meet my eyes whilst doing his job. The professor reassured me and examined my charts, and then I was wheeled into the operation theatre. I was off to sleep in a few seconds and woke up in the recovery room with a strong itch on my abdomen and an instant desire to urinate. I wanted to get up to go to the loo and then realized where I was. I now understood what post-operative amnesia meant. I felt terribly confused.

The nurse came up to me and she wanted me to urinate into a urine bottle. I was not going to do that! I was far too macho to do it in the bottle.

I politely kept the bottle next to me, and when she was not looking, just hobbled into the toilet. Wow. The pain in my abdomen was searing. I was suffering from young- doctor-who-knows-it-all syndrome; I had to learn to swallow my pride. There were no subsequent trips to the toilet for the next few hours.

I had my recovery planned at my mom's aunt's house, which was not very far from the hospital. There was not much of an age difference between my aunt and my mother, my aunt was the youngest sibling in her family. I lovingly called her *Maasi*, a term reserved for a mother's sister. She was one of my most loving relatives. She always had a smile on her face, was calm, exuded self-confidence, and sang bhajans daily. All the members of her family followed a particular spiritual leader, whose pictures were in all of the rooms of the house. Perhaps it was this relationship with her guru that made her so calm and collected. Whatever be the case, she seemed much calmer than my mother.

The days went by too quickly. My batch mates visited me daily and I had a couple of girls from my batch visit too. Wow, it felt nice to be a bit pampered.

In the last couple of years before graduation, I finally did find my soul mate in a girl whom I knew from my own high school. We dated nearly daily during the first few months of our relationship. The world seemed so magical and special. But we fought too, and a lot. Our love and passion grew. I just could not sleep at night, as I would be constantly thinking about her. The agitation receded only when I saw her. We talked for hours on end every time that we met. We both were at the same level of training but in different medical colleges. She was also a resident of her college hostel.

Her college was special, in a way. It was the one and only medical college in the world dedicated solely to female students. It was very clear that her college dean was very protective of her wards. There was a lot of security around the hostel with tall iron walls and gates constantly manned by guards. No men were allowed into the female residences. It would be Herculean to cross over those gates at any time of the day or night.

Every day that I arrived at the hostel gates on my two-wheeled scooter, her name was announced by the security guard over the hostel public address system. I knew she was embarrassed that the guy on the blue scooter had arrived again. I suspect that her batch mates teased her. She would frequently come out blushing, and she would sometimes be angry. But a few smiles from me and we would both be blissfully happy in each other's company. I shared my deepest thoughts with her, talked about the past, planned for the future – stuff that most people in love do.

It seemed that we had just started to date (it had been a few months) when she informed me that we might have to let her parents know that we were seeing each other, and we were committed. I was told that her parents had recently received a marriage proposal from THE physician son of another general in the army. Now that was very interesting. I was told that "he" was already "settled" in the USA and had been an internal medicine resident for the last couple of years.

It was time for us to make a decision about where our relationship was going. I knew I had her heart, but I also knew that she respected her parents and their wishes a lot. We agreed that it would be best to be honest with our parents and make them aware that we were seriously invested in our relationship. Then it happened. I proposed to her on the auditorium steps of her medical college where so many hearts had been broken as well as mended.

She said yes!

Now came the gruelling part: she broke the news to her parents and they wished to see me immediately. It was time to grill the twenty-three-year-old boy who wished to marry their youngest, twenty-three-year-old daughter. My girlfriend seemed so relaxed, that it helped me feel calm too. Her parents flew in from Calcutta a few days later and I got interviewed for around half an hour. It was likely the longest half hour that I ever faced in my life. I did not know them and they did not know me. I had to show my confidence, yet not come across as over-confident. I had to talk about myself and my family, my hopes and aspirations. I had to show that I was a general's son who knew how to talk and walk. I hoped I came across as calm and collected.

The feedback that I got later was that her mom felt that I was too young. Well, indeed, that I was. However, she was twenty-three too and they had been thinking of marrying her off. That was my only defence. We both had made up our minds to be with each other. It was up to them to bless us as a couple or we were going to get married anyway.

As things turned out we got married within six months and with the blessings of our parents. It was a proper Indian wedding with lots of pomp and regality; my mom would not have had it any other way. The two families seem to be open enough to accommodate each other's needs and intricacies.

My wife and I moved into a small room in the college hostel. We both got into specialist training, had our first daughter when we both were twenty-seven and within a couple of years were on our journey to England to take research positions. Time was moving quickly and things were going as per "plan." But things change. That is the only thing constant about life, isn't it?

England felt completely strange to us. It was a brave new world for us, and our two and a half-year-old daughter. After having been exposed to the West mostly through Hollywood with a lot of action and fantasy movies, Western advertisements for Coca-Cola, and MTV where everything was bright, jovial, and sunny, we were shocked to find ourselves in this city in the north of England, which was cold, drab, and felt lonely. Compared to the hustle and bustle of Delhi we hardly found anyone on the streets. What we saw was not pretty. There was rowdiness, misbehaviour, foul language, people urinating on the streets at night, and worst of all, racism, which was obvious. The television blared all the time that the U.K. did not endorse or believe in racism. Perhaps our experience was being coloured by the neighbourhood that we were living in. But that was the only place we could afford. Our research posts paid meagrely and it was an expensive country.

We were constantly calculating how much the same thing would have cost in India. We could not afford a car. We had wanted our daughter to go to a private nursery, as we were used to in India, but the cost of childcare was exorbitant so we stuck with her going to the local council nursery instead. She stopped speaking within a few months of going to the nursery, even though she used to speak in Hindi all the time in India. We had no option but to send her to a private nursery where she would hopefully get more one-on-one attention. She had always been very special to us, not only because she was our first child, but because she was the one that we came very close to losing.

I remembered the day she was born, the world felt so beautiful and special. However, within a few hours of her birth we were alarmed to find that she was just not perking up, and not interested in nursing. I alerted my paediatric resident colleague that there was something wrong. He placed her in an incubator and she was put on an intravenous line and antibiotics. They suspected that she had developed some sort of a bacterial infection during the delivery. The most nerve-racking days of our lives were ahead of us. Morning, evening, and night we stayed outside the neonatal ICU, hoping to hear that she had started to perk up. But she would remain listless, without any improvement for four days. Slowly, though, she started to recover and by the end of the seventh day she was taking to her mom's breast.

I just could not ever let this daughter of mine out of my sight.

To see her struggling again in our land of fantasy, in this wonderful country of the Queen, was heart breaking. We had to consider asking my parents to fly over from India just to be with her while we both were at work, but we knew that they would not fit into our small house. Additionally, the flights from India were way too expensive for me, or for what my dad's army pay would have been able to cover. Mom had retired some time ago and she had no pension. Additionally, both parents would have felt so different and likely embarrassed to see us in this small little house of ours. Dad was a general and I knew that he had a retinue of staff, luxuriously large houses with a front and rear gardens, and a couple of cars always available to him, all provided by the Indian Army. He was not going to fit in taking public transport in England. The cost of a bus ticket in Newcastle was equivalent to filling up our car in India with gas for the whole month.

We had to face the facts that the high costs of food and the atrocious rent on the small, two-bedroom apartment would hardly leave us with much money to spare. It was our wish, perhaps now a fantasy, to visit and see the rest of the United Kingdom and Europe. That was not going to be possible. Waves of unhappiness and depression started to hit me. I believed that I could not let my wife know how I had started to feel responsible for the destruction of our fantasy.

We had never felt so painfully different before, because of our skin colour, our English accents and the general way we did things. The staff at the psychiatric research unit of the hospital where we worked was really good, but we noticed that there was clear demarcation in so many obvious as well as subtle ways. The white senior house officer would go out with his mates for a drink after work, and they would have their own parties. They would speak about football games, about which we knew nothing and their interest in art and music was so much different from ours.

I could not let that isolation happen. I knew how important it was to try to be a part of the culture so that we could feel included.

In the end, we were extremely lucky to be indoctrinated into English culture by, believe it or not, a Scottish senior resident. She took it upon herself to teach us how things ticked. Her presence was so comforting, and her smile and laughter so calming.

At her suggestion, we moved out of our research posts and prepared for psychiatry residency positions, which paid three times what the research posts offered. She suggested places to eat and how to eat. We learnt so much about the nitty-gritty of the differences between the English and the Scots. Slowly we started to adapt ourselves to our new life. Isn't it interesting that when you feel you are at your lowest ebb, the world again changes and you find yourself in the hands of a saviour?

We moved into a much larger house where we could plan our second child and could call it a home. Things were starting to perk up a bit more. We had regular parties at home; I no longer denied myself alcohol or meat. My parents were able to visit yearly now. I really started to feel calm and loved spending time with my patients. My level of comfort in speaking with them really improved. My "difficult" accent turned into an asset, as I would, in my mind, call it the Queen's accent while they had a Geordie accent. I started to participate in outdoor activities much more, including travelling, hiking, taking the family out to nature walks, and visiting a number of cities in England and Europe on small getaways. The bank balance was starting to look much healthier too. The dream was coming true. Overall, the quality of our lives seemed so much better.

Sadly though, things were really not so good between my wife and me. We frequently fought over little things. We both loved each other, we both knew that, but there were certain days of the month where we just could not see eye to eye. If there was something in particular that I needed to talk about, involving life in India, it would veer off in the direction of her parents or her siblings and I would soon be cringing and wondering why I had brought up the topic. Money started to dominate discussions. We had made a couple of real estate investments in India that unhappily turned sour.

We planned an extension on our garage and after due diligence selected a particular builder. My wife was pregnant with our second child by then and we needed the additional bedroom to be built soon. It was early December and we had our annual trip to India planned out. In full faith we handed over a substantial down payment to the builder so that he could continue the work over the three weeks that we were away.

On our return in January, we were devastated to see that no work had begun on the bedroom. That was the last straw. It felt like we just could not hold on to our money.

I found out later that the builder had suffered a series of misfortunes in having lost his son-in-law, who was his business partner. He had also broken his arm and had filed for bankruptcy. All this had happened in the three weeks that we were away. I subsequently put in a request through the Small Claims Court for my money and I contacted a collection agency to help me recover the losses, but I felt, or rather I knew with a gut feeling, that nothing would come of my efforts. Intuition wells up in us when we most need it.

We did not receive a single penny of our money back. By then, we'd lost three thousand pounds on our house in England and around seventeen thousand on our investments in India.

We found a new builder soon and though we knew we were paying much more than the market rate, we had no other option but to use him. At least this builder lived in the same neighbourhood as us. Additionally, his father was an ex-police officer so we thought that he came from a good upbringing and would have values to honour the contract and complete the job. In my mind I was comparing and contrasting the two builders, as if by simply knowing of their backgrounds I could predict the future of our home. I needed to have some level of faith that this time things would not go wrong.

Our second daughter arrived in the world and the extension got completed just shy of a couple of months late. We finally did have a nursery for her!

However, the largest shock was waiting in the background.

A few years earlier, in India, my father had bravely and successfully gone through a radiotherapy course for a small cancerous tumour on his tongue. I had felt a bit anxious about it but was strangely proud of my medical skills, since I had discovered the tumour on his first trip to the U.K. He was on a tourist visa and he would not be eligible for regular National Health Service hospital treatment. I remember he had been only ten days into his visit when he asked me to examine a lymph node underneath his jaw.

I felt so forlorn and unhappy that I had to give him the bad news that this was not just any regular ulcer on the tongue; I could also feel a hard, non-painful lymph node under his jaw. That meant only one thing: cancer.

He took the news exceptionally well and did not seem to mind cutting short his trip. A few days later, he returned to India, with my mother. The very next day, he had a biopsy and the report confirmed my suspicions of cancer. He was just fifty-six at that time. I tried to reassure my mother that oral cancer was the most treatable form of cancer; radiotherapy and surgery had a very high cure rate. Still, in the back of my mind I was also aware that my father did not have any of the classical risk factors for causing the cancer in the first place. He did not smoke, did not chew tobacco, and there was no history of any cancers in his family. I did, though, remember that he'd had frequent, recurrent, non-healing ulcers on his tongue after his posting in Sri Lanka. I kept this information to myself, as mother would have been extremely scared if she heard of my suspicions. My father went through a course of radiotherapy without any complications. His tumour regressed and the lymph node was no longer palpable.

Six years later the cancer returned with a vengeance. I was in the middle of my higher specialist training being trained to become a geriatric psychiatrist. I wanted to help, to just be next to him, as much as I could, but also knew that I could not leave my training in the middle to be with him for too long. At least I was comforted to just observe his faith, on the phone, on Skype. He remained a true soldier.

He went through repeated courses of radiotherapy and experimental chemotherapy without any complaint. My mother's rigor and faith started to grow even more. I heard from my cousins that she had a strange glow on her face as she nursed him through all the procedures.

I visited as much as I could. He would just look at me and smile. He could no longer speak as the tumour was progressing fast. Repeated MRI scans of the head and neck area confirmed that the therapies were not working. He knew that he did not have much time to live, but whenever I visited him he wrote down for me on a piece of paper that he knew he would be just fine. I thought, or rather was very sure, that he was in denial. It made no other sense from the psychological point of view. He knew he was dying, so why deny this fact except to maybe help us embrace accepting his loss better, I guess. My knowledge of psychiatry made me believe so. My mother started to stay up through the nights praying at the altar at home, going twice a day to the local temple, and offering donations to various religious charities. She frequently broke down when I came home. I knew she found my presence comforting.

He had stopped eating a long time ago, as he just could not swallow. The mass was growing at the back of his tongue and pushing the airway forward as well. He needed a tracheostomy, an artificial and permanent opening of his airway, and that meant a lot of cleaning of secretions day and night. Mother prepared all his feeds, five times a day, and helped suck out the secretions at least twenty times a day.

On my last trip, he showed me all his accounting files. He had sold off all his stock and bonds a few months earlier and transferred all the money to saving accounts. He had kept a detailed account of all the transactions, which would have put any accountant or bookkeeper to shame.

He survived the recurrence for two years but then passed away one day while I was at work. I somehow knew that something wrong was going to happen that day and then I heard my phone go off. My mother just said that he was no longer with us, and to come home. I caught the earliest available flight. I had dreaded this moment. The eldest son had to do the last rites as per Hindu traditions. I was back at home sixteen hours from the time the news had reached me. I remember just seeing his body. I could not bear to see his face.

I was amazed to see so many of his friends and relatives had turned up. An army truck had been decorated with marigold garlands to take him to the cremation grounds. The rest of my memories of the events are a bit of a blur. I was walking along dazed. I remember, though, being able to sleep soundly in that house for the first time in two years. Mother also rested well that night.

I broke tradition and offered to organize a power point presentation of his life through the eyes of his two sons. In traditional Hindu culture or in the Indian Army no one ever organizes a memorial. Tradition demands that we just let go after somebody passes away. Nevertheless, both my brother and I felt compelled to talk with my father's friends and family about his achievements. We felt we owed this to our father. He had done so much for us; all we needed to do was organize a few things to make the presentation memorable. We spent a bit of time scouring through old photograph albums, scanned some pictures, and prepared a presentation that I have never had the courage to look at again. I was told later that everyone in the room felt extremely moved. His closest friends spoke so highly of him. In their eyes he was a blessed soul who had been the most upright officer that they had ever met. My cousins mentioned about his strong filial ties, and my brother and I spoke about him being there for us whenever we needed him and teaching us so many wonderful values.

I cried every day for the next few years. But never in front of my wife or my two daughters. I was too proud to show it.

Despair, despondency, irritability, lack of interest seemed to swathe me occasionally, but I continued to keep it to myself, waiting for some miracle to happen. And that did happen over the next few years. I found my faith and life has been transformed.

CHAPTER 3. Why Should We All Get on the Spiritual Path?

NOW LET'S FAST-FORWARD TO THE PRESENT. I AM PRIVILEGED AND extremely lucky to work as a consultant geriatric psychiatrist in a large secondary-care hospital in London, Canada. I am very grateful to have been given the opportunity to do research on various clinical and biological aspects related to mental health. Additionally, I have the opportunity to meet, assess, and treat people with mental health issues both as inpatients and outpatients.

Notice that I used the term mental health "issues" rather than "diagnoses." The stigma around discussing and resolving our mental health issues remains very strong. Most of these issues arise from our minds' inability to cope with stress. We need to accept that in our modern lives we all face situations that could potentially cause us to be stressed. When stress, which is a state of mind, persists for a period of time, it has a chance of becoming a disorder. In the rest of this book if a reference is made to a condition like depression, anxiety, and so on and so forth, I am inviting the reader to think of this as a state of mind where we feel depressed or anxious; not necessarily the disorder where such states of mind can become persistent to the point where the quality of life is severely affected.

Let us first accept that each and every one of us goes through difficult feelings on a day-to-day basis. One wonderful advantage that I have found for being on the spiritual path is that I personally notice that worry, stress, and depressive and anxious feelings no longer seem to take control over me. I try to always be an observer of such thoughts rather than an experiencer of difficult thoughts. I have now mostly learnt how to make the intellect keep the mind in check, being constantly vigilant that the mind and the senses have the tendency to pull me down.

I invite everybody to follow the path of Vedantic spirituality, if you have stress or not, if you have mental health issues, or if you have a mental disorder. The knowledge and practices of Vedanta are a step-by-step approach to allow us to relax, to be in charge of our thoughts, and to live naturally.

CHAPTER 4. Depression

I AM NOW GOING TO SHARE FURTHER THOUGHTS AND IDEAS AS TO why we all have depressive thoughts and how Vedanta-based spirituality can help with depressive symptoms/disorder. Additionally, I shall bring forth concise information on the science behind spiritual practices and the wonderful research findings that are coming through.

Needless to say, it is crucial to recognize that if people are having severe symptoms of depression, which might include paranoid thoughts of people trying to harm them; suicidal thoughts with the intention of taking their own lives; and losing complete interest in life where they are isolating themselves completely – these people need the professional help available from a family doctor and/or a psychiatrist. There is clear evidence that in moderate to severe depression antidepressants work extremely well and they need to be taken, at least during the times of the biggest dips in our moods. A person in the grips of such a severe condition of the mind might not be able to practice various spiritual techniques such as meditation. Saying this, in our own ongoing research work on elderly people with clinical depression, even of moderate severity, we are finding significant benefits with *Sahaj Samadhi* Meditation which belongs to the category of automatic self-transcending meditation. I shall describe this briefly, later.

This book is not a treatise on antidepressants and their benefits or side effects. The biological approach to the management of mental health conditions has been the bane of modern psychiatry till recently. We have forgotten the benefits of human contact and spirituality to help us identify our true nature and of recognizing these options to help us stay healthy.

All spiritual belief systems suggest that the road to joy is from within. However, we are constantly looking for it outside us; in the work that we do, in our families, and in the material things that we consume. The desire to find happiness outside of ourselves takes us away from our true nature. We get agitated and start feeling low and depressed at the drop of a hat. Our egos and sense organs maintain our desires and when we don't achieve our desires we get ignorantly caught up and remain depressed.

For a typical person this is the story of someone living in this world: When we are school age, Mom and Dad help us to get to school, and we are busy with our peers and don't have the time to start a spiritual journey. As we get older, we are busy trying to receive higher education, finding a loved one, marriage, and then kids. We then get too busy in our jobs. As we get towards our middle age, we are still waiting to find the right time to start our spiritual journey as life has become horribly complex with no time for ourselves, let alone for meditation and other spiritual practices. Time goes on and we become older; our social circle becomes smaller due to death in friends and loved ones, we become isolated, and we can't seem to find the happiness within ourselves. It is then perhaps too late.

We had always imagined that as we got older we would have "the time" to feel joyful! Where did the time go? We start becoming acutely conscious that we have only a short duration of time left to live, and we start feeling desperate and anxious, trying to find happiness. Why did we have to wait our whole lives to find that happiness? And finally, death comes to all of us. It is the most basic truth of our lives – nobody lives forever.

The certainty about the spiritual path is that you can and will find happiness right now; you don't have to wait till you are older to start your journey. Open your eyes and you will find happiness in every moment of your life right now. It is never too late.

Have you noticed that we feel upset when somebody does not do things the way that we want him or her to? You come back from a tiring day at work and want to unwind but realize that there is so much still to do to keep the household going. Children need attention, but your partner is busy doing some chores. Children want to share their stories, and there's dinner to be prepared, the kitchen to be cleaned, the garbage to be thrown out.... the list keeps going on and on. You heave a long sigh and feel drained even before you start to do the stuff that needs to be done. You become irritable because of that perceived inappropriate or snide remark from your loved one, or you could start blaming the person at work who made you feel like that; the boss who just does not understand your worth and is purposefully trying to show you up. You grab a bottle of beer or wine and hope that the alcohol will help you unwind and forget about the miseries that are undeniably there. You switch on the TV or look up your social media and read the news and feel the whole world is coming crashing down. Everybody appears to be a narcissist or evil or a terrorist. You just don't find the purpose or the point of this world. The kids are put to sleep and you try to have a conversation with your partner. He/she has similar stories to tell, which echo with your experience. You feel miserable in hearing this but do try to offer some support to each other. You go off to sleep and another day starts and the cycle continues.

Does this sound familiar? This could be what a typical evening for an adult with a family might look like. Of course not every adult has a family, nor does everyone have a job, but you might find similarities to the above story in your own experiences.

So what do we do to make us closer to our nature?

The first step is to stop thinking about your work as soon as you have left the office. Distract yourself by a pleasant thought, remind yourself to be grateful that you are alive and inhaling this wonderful air, having what ever you have. Just let go of all your thoughts, including expectations and desires. Just sit in the car/bus for a few minutes before driving off. If you can, close your eyes. If not, with open eyes focus on your breath. The breath is the only thing that is constant when you are alive, so just observe your breath. Take a minute or so to feel the air going through the nostrils, into your lungs and then feel it coming out through the nostrils. Feel the warmth of the incoming air and the coolness of the air coming out. With each breath recognize that every incoming breath offers you Divine energy and strength and the outgoing breath makes you feel relaxed and calm. Just be at peace with these feelings. When you are ready, then just open your eyes and proceed on your journey. On your way do not think about what you did/did not do or try, and don't judge either yourself or the person about whom you are thinking. Instead, bring a gentle smile to your face and recognize that whatever happened has already happened and you do not have any control over the past. Thinking about it now has already made your present move into the past. So let us live in the present and observe the beauty of the world around us right now. Observe another person in a car and smile to yourself, thinking about being around another human being who is also a bundle of energy, thoughts, emotions, and desires just like you. Try to find the connectedness rather than the difference. Do not blame his driving habits if he cuts across your path. Perhaps he is genuinely in a hurry to get home as some matter needs his urgent attention. Perhaps his day has been horrible and he is trying to run away from it, literally. Do not blame him for the way he is behaving; nothing and no one can touch you in that blissful state of yours. Rather, try to bring up feelings of compassion towards him. Say to yourself that this person does not know that his driving might have potentially hurt someone. He is just ignorant of his actions.

If the weather permits, open the windows and feel the fresh air caressing your face, your skin, and your body. The wind is a source of Divine energy and will replenish you. If you cannot open the window, just feel the air conditioner's wind coming onto your face and body and be thankful that you have a job to go to and money to pay for the public transport or your car, and let all your apprehension and worrisome thoughts melt away.

Gratitude for simply being alive dispels the cloud of ego sitting on our intellects.

When you arrive home you will be fully refreshed. Keep that smile on your face and everyone will smile back at you, guaranteed. Be attentive to your kids and their stories and you will feel fully energized. Start preparing dinner with a feeling of gratitude that you have a kitchen to go to, ingredients with which you can prepare a meal, working electricity, and a warm house and you will start feeling that you are already in Heaven. Use the chopping board with lightness in your action.

a) The Role of Desires

Most spiritual pathways and religions mention that our desires are the root cause of feelings of guilt, depression, worry, and even psychosis. Vedanta shows that if we, at all times, are in touch with the supreme Self; grateful for just living; living in constant awe and wondering about this creation; and dispassionate about the everything that we do, then desires do not even arise. However, in our non-enlightened states we succumb to our desires for each and every thing that our sense organs demand. We go down the slippery slope of attachment to the fruits of our action and feel depressed when our desires are not completed.

Let us understand the relationship between desires, our minds, and our feelings a little bit more.

As we live, walk, talk, and do our daily duties, every moment that we are doing something, we are utilizing our sense organs. Whatever we put in our mouths seems to dictate how we are going to feel in the next few seconds. If the food tastes horrible, indeed we will feel awful. However, if the food tastes good, we want more and more of it till our tummies burst! Similarly, you can extrapolate the extent of other sense organs' control over you, be it touch (sex, hot, cold, etc.), smell (pleasant versus unpleasant), hearing (pleasant versus unpleasant remarks), and seeing (pleasant versus unpleasant). We all seek the pleasant so much that we get enamoured by it to a point that we get agitated when we do not receive it immediately. I am sure when you read this you will become conscious of things that you are attracted or even possibly addicted to, perhaps alcohol, a type of food, sex, etc. However, let us not fret about the control that these things have over us. We can learn how to let go of our desires through the knowledge below.

Let us first of all accept that whatever we acquire seems to satisfy our senses for only a short time. We can never get a sense of belonging with that thing. It might make us feel happy for a few days, or perhaps a few weeks, and, then like any child, we become bored with it and want something else. Have we not noticed that a child says that he/she is bored with a toy very quickly? Does that not give us an important clue that all things acquired will lead to us rejecting them very quickly and will make us feel unhappy and sad shortly afterwards?

If my mind is constantly being titillated by my sense organs, I know I can't cut off my mind from the rest of me. How can I then stop being a slave to my desires?

Perhaps this Vedantic equation might help.

Happiness= *Desires entertained/Desires attained.*

So if I wish to increase my level of happiness then I need to either reduce the number of desires that I entertain or increase the number of desires attained. All desires cannot be attained, so won't I be better off not to entertain desires that trouble me? The next best gadget and the next model of the car that I like, are my desires. You can think of all the other desires that your mind conjures up. That list can be long or short. Recognise that these thoughts are being generated by the mind, which by nature is fickle. Your intellect, which is rooted to the Supreme Self talks to you and says, "Hey my dear fellow, what is the point of having that next iPhone when the current one is working just fine?"

We might say to that inner calling, "Nah, it is just a phone, what is the big deal? I want it. It looks good and has all those cool and nice new features. I don't want to look stupid in front of other people who might have this new model." And we keep going on, trying to justify our attempts to complete our desires.

But the innermost part of your intellect is talking to you, albeit in a small voice: "I have provided for you. Think how you can help others instead of fulfilling another of your desires. Helping others will make you happier and for longer." But we negate that thought completely, we succumb to our desires, buy the new phone, feel happy for a short period, and then it is just another piece of equipment. The happiness that we initially found from owning the technology is now gone. Everybody seems to have the new phone. Now you compare and contrast and think of which app to download and which one is better! The list goes on for wishful thinking, procurement of materialistic items, and feelings of unhappiness!

Think of any measureable thing that you wish to have, recognize that it is a desire, laugh at how your desires are erupting, intellectualize that you do not need it, and with a little bit of self-effort, just let go of your desire. The letting-go part is crucial. It only takes a few seconds to let go. We have to start inculcating the habit of letting go. The person who is on the journey will soon realize that the Divine shall provide what is needed. He might provide more than is needed as well. These are all opportunities to give back to the community more, so that you can be even happier and joy becomes a part of your nature.

So another equation could be:

Joy or Bliss = *Giving to others with no expectations of being thanked.*

Simple. No addition, multiplication, or division.

I was privileged to hear another secret from a learned person. He said to me that a seeker can't completely be bereft of desires. Indeed our minds are attached to our sense organs, and these organs have only one function – to remind us of the love flowing through us for the Divine. These sensations are just an expression of that eternal love. It is we who convert them into desires or wants because of our egos, peer pressure, and our memories of the past. If these desires are repressed, they further blossom as a weed with deep roots. If we try to pull the weed out it keeps returning, because the roots go really deep.

If we must desire something, let us all have a desire instead for the ultimate truth; the higher calling, i.e. finding and being with your true Selves. Then our minds, which are fickle, will have no choice but to let go of our lower, vile desires. It is up to us to choose wisely. Love your Self every moment of your life and you will be so much calmer. Love your Self with the intention of being one with it. The Divine placed these sense organs so that we can appreciate the bliss that comes from attaching to Him. So desire the Divine at every moment and you will find bliss becomes your body, mind, and intellect. You will then not get caught up with your desires.

As you start to let go of your desires, you will start noticing many things that are currently wrong with society, over which you do not have much direct control. You will notice that growing up in this materialistic, capitalistic world has forced us to think that we have to make ourselves look and be more accomplished than others. It is a fact that competition can be healthy if taken with the right spirit and frame of mind. So let us all celebrate our differences and yet accept the commonalities. Let us always remember that wealth-generation, through conducting a business, has occurred with the growth of the human intellect over thousands of years. Wealth-generation has never been looked down upon by any religion or spiritual belief. However, in this modern world one up-manship has rather started to be celebrated. Let us not get affected by these herd behaviours. Rather, let us find eternal bliss in just accepting that at the core we are all one who care for the growth of humanity. If we inculcate this attitude of the betterment of everyone, a desire to be better than the other person just falls away. We become our natural selves and more productive at our own work. We might even become better than our supposed enemies at work. Even so, let us never look down upon the person who is not doing as good as we are.

When you go to work with such a positive attitude, you will start noticing more people who are smiling. These are indeed the expressions of the Divine. A genuine smile makes us feel completely hooked and tantalized. Hook on to that smile and thank the Divinity in the person, and you will feel the need to smile as well. The mind will feel so much happier.

Let us develop the habit of smiling even when it feels artificial; it will soon become our own nature. As we have grown older we have lost our true nature by being bombarded by a lot of information indicating that there are differences that exist between each of us. In the name of religion we differentiate each other's beliefs and values. In the name of colour we are subtly racist. In the name of pride and achievement we try to show our houses, spouses, children, and technological products proudly. Let us be more contented and grateful for what we have.

Who gave us all that we have? If man has made machines, those machines are made of materials, which came from Him. So let us rejoice in acknowledging the power of Him and feel in love with Him. If He made us look different and separate, that has been done for us to learn the concept of beauty in diversity. So what is the point of comparing ourselves with another human? Compare yourself with everything else too: That piece of wood, which just stays there but provides you a table so that you can work and eat your food on. That bird, which chirps in the morning every day, to help you wake up. That blade of grass, which is so beautifully green under the sunlight and sparks up looking even more beautiful when drops of rain fall on it. Your daughter or son who loves to show you his/her achievement in school or college. That enemy of yours who allows you to learn that hatred is a feeling that is only momentary and passes away. Next time you are with your perceived enemy, try to look into his/her eyes with compassion and you will find a much deeper connection with him/her. Remember that if we see someone as an enemy, or someone has a character trait that we find to be negative; then it is time that we let go of our negative attitudes towards him or her. The more accepting that we are, the less the world seems bothersome. The more positivity that we try to find in others, the more positive we become. Let us hence start by showing compassion and love more for the person that we really hate, not for the person who we naturally like.

I have heard people say that they do not get along well with a particular person, as if there are some vibes that the person emanates, which make us despise them. Just by pure logic, emotions are always opposite; love and hate, happiness and sadness, agitation and relaxation. However, our natural state is of a depth that is beyond these opposites. It is calm, serene, and joyful. When we display compassion and pure unadulterated love, then the dual nature of the emotions just dissipates. Compassion is like a natural state, a jewel that we all have, but which shines brighter as we grind our egos away. Then compassion shines like a diamond spreading a light, which becomes visible to everyone who looks in our direction.

b) Ego Dissolution

As I go further on my spiritual journey, I read, realize, and reflect that the biggest impediment to my spiritual growth is still my ego. However, just a couple of years ago, during my early days on my spiritual journey, I thought the ego was useful. This incorrect assumption was engendered from reading psychiatric textbooks; I had read that the ego is the building block that helps us differentiate one from the other. I am separate from my mother; I am different from my sibling and my father, and so on and so forth. If we were to further reflect on this, we all know that as a child grows, the ego helps it to differentiate itself from its friends, teachers, uncles, and aunts. So, I had learnt that having an ego is essential and very useful.

The problem with my limited learning till that time was that I had not realized that the ego is also the biggest bane of a human being. I had learnt how to distance myself from narcissistic and antisocial personality-disordered people, as I knew that their egos were too inflated. Little did I realize that I was trying to make myself separate from them. It was my ego preventing me from getting closer to them. Yes, I did get hurt every time that I spoke with someone with a very big ego. So why get close to him or her? Simple, unsaid reasoning that I had picked up from my colleagues and seniors!

How wrong I was.

I now know that every time that I am not letting myself interact with someone who has a big ego, I am hurting that person and I am being hurt too because my ego gets hurt as I am not able to help him or her. And in this process I feel guilty about not being a good enough psychiatrist. Over the last little while, I have learned how important it is to respect and accept teach and every person the way that they are. Showing courtesy, dignity, and love is all I need to show and it helps me grow with everyone. All the time that I am with them, I will take a pledge that I will be ever mindful of the basic qualities required of a good human being. Then only will I be a good enough physician. I will be mindful that I never say to myself that I am a good physician, because that itself is an ego-boosting statement. The only reason that I am working in this job is because I have an opportunity to give. If at any time I think self-adulatory or congratulatory thoughts about being a good physician, my ego gets boosted and I go on a different plane than the person sitting next to me. If someone is trying to show me his deepest worries, apprehensions, or desires, I shall listen and be with him or her. I will not allow my intellect and mind be taken for a ride. I will not let my ego distance me from the person and thwart the therapeutic relationship. I shall be there when someone needs me. I will never react or respond to inappropriate remarks or demands, because such comments and mannerisms are designed to validate the ego in the person sitting next to me, as well as in me. Let me remain strong in this resolution. That is my prayer.

I remember just a little while ago I was walking towards the ward with a medical student and a resident. One of the program residents pointed out that I was lucky to have a medical student and a resident both completing a rotation with me at the same time. This resident felt that teaching them would make my ego grow. She referred to the students as Ego Boosting Units. I remember smiling back and saying to this resident that I looked forward to teaching students as Ego Bursting Units instead. That resident looked very surprised to hear this comment. She must have said to herself that Dr. Vasudev had gone mad!

Our concept of the need to have a big ego to survive this materialistic world has become so ingrained in us that if somebody even suggests that we should not have a large ego, we look at him or her in a strange way. I have now learnt that teaching, when done without any sense of attachment, reward, or expectations is the best and the quickest way for spiritual growth of that individual. The act of teaching anyone without any expectation of a reward of any sort, helps us grow spiritually. Hence, teaching is the best profession for a person to grow on the spiritual path, as long as his or her intellect keeps the ego in check.

Everybody is a teacher, a guru, as we are all here to teach someone at some time and we are also here to learn the journey of how to get liberated. May He give us the courage and the fortitude that we are able to do both these activities (learning and teaching) with so much courage, that come what may, we will be reposed in the faith in the Divine at every moment of our lives.

I am not going to provide any more examples of the ego and its constant undoing, because that will likely be a long thesis. Additionally, the reader is likely aware of the power of the ego from instances in their own lives. What is more important is to learn how we can let go of the ego. Do note that I do not say that we should destroy the ego. If we try to destroy the ego, it becomes even stronger in rebellion as it has become so very ingrained in us.

Vedanta shows that we can let go of the ego through four easy steps. 1) Knowledge that we are part of and are the same creation. 2) Selfless work. 3) Devotion to the Supreme Self. 4) Dispassion. We will explore these concepts again and again as they are vitally important to our spiritual growth. And on days when you know that you are feeling hurt, because your ego is hurt, root yourself to this knowledge again and again. If you are sincere in your journey and want to find enlightenment, your ego will dissipate. It is guaranteed.

c) Memory

I have noticed another phenomenon that causes great grief to lots of people. That is our memories. People try to find pleasure in the past; how good the good old days were, how many friends they had, how the children used to look so cute and cuddly, what beautiful bodies that they had. And then they contrast this with their present moment. The kids have grown big, they are so busy in their activities, they have left home; the friends have moved on; their bodies look old and fat etc. etc. So it seems the purpose of having a memory is to make our present moment look bad and sad!

Now let us try to think of this spiritually.

Having a memory can be a blessing as well as a hindrance. A man is forgetful of his true nature. We will learn soon about man's true nature, which is *Aham Brahmasmi*. This means "I am Divine." Our Divine Self is the purest form of us, which has been coloured by time, tainted by memory, gets regularly bashed up by our emotions, and is camouflaged by the ego. This forgetfulness of our true nature is likely the root cause of all problems and suffering in life. The very remembrance of one's nature, which is godliness, brings freedom in life. Here, memory is your best friend. The purpose of spiritual knowledge is to remind you of your true nature.

In the Vedantic Holy Book, *Bhagvad Gita*, Arjuna, when faced with fighting his family for the ill deeds that they had committed, finds himself immobile and not able to go to war with them because of memories of the good deeds that they had done. Lord Krishna provides him the knowledge and Arjuna responds, "I got back my memory. Now I have realized and will do as you say." He then had the courage, vigour, and strength to go to war with his own family. He had forgotten his true nature and felt unnerved to a point where he just did not feel capable of fighting the war, though he was the most skilful warrior of his time. Only with Lord Krishna showing him his true nature, did Arjuna feel capable of fighting the war. Memory is indeed a blessing and your best friend when you realize your true nature.

Memory is also a hindrance when it does not let you be free of events; pleasant or unpleasant. You have read about the five sensations and how we can get attracted to them. Having a pleasant event in the current moment can create a craving for more of this sensation. Or we might become jealous when we see that someone has more than we have. We forget our true natures and have unhealthy thoughts and feelings in our minds. So the memory is both a blessing and a hindrance, depending on whether you remember your nature or you are stuck with events in time and space.

So just accept this aspect of memory – it serves no major purpose but to help you always remember your true nature.

They say charity begins at home. This sentence has such a deep meaning. The word "home" could be your own body as well as the people living in close physical proximity to you. We need to show charity to both. To stay on the spiritual path and grow, disciplining ourselves so that our bodies remain healthy is crucial. A diet that is light in calories and fat content makes us feel elevated in spirit, and helps to preserve discipline with our sleep habits, with exercising our bodies regularly, and with maintaining good physical hygiene. All of these disciplines help us to have good mental hygiene too. Too frequently when we feel depressed we let go of these things that our body needs. We become lethargic, we eat unwisely, we do not sleep properly, and then our energy levels feel low. But by forcing our bodies to maintain these habits, depressive thoughts and feelings have less of a chance to establish a hold on us. Our bodies are adaptable to what we put in them, the number of hours that we allow them to sleep and the smell that we allow them to have. By keeping the body clean, we are forcing it to accept the goodness in our cores, our own Self.

There is a reason that people go through a "middle age crisis," the "seven-year itch" and so on and so forth. We get so accustomed to the people that we are living with that they have memories of what makes us react. We also have memories of when we reacted and responded, and we just keep going in circles. For us to grow in spirit, it is we who must change – and not the people, places, or things around us. When we change who or what we are within our hearts, our lives follow suit and change too. Hence, reflecting on what we do, and more importantly on how we think on a regular basis, is the only basis for growth. Our memories of the past can help us move forward. Yes, we are creatures of habit. But habits can and should change if we have to grow spiritually. When a person irritates you, feel the emotions well up as they have done before, but catch the emotion and the thoughts before they get to the crescendo. Do not react immediately – take a deep breath and then just let it go. If you respond to the irritation and shout or become upset yourself, you have made things bad. The other person is going to react as well and the situation is likely going to worsen. Keep your memories in check and the world will look and feel beautiful.

At this point, let me share a life-changing incident from my life. A couple of years ago, I attended a program called the Happiness Program in which we were made to sit in a group of four, with people whom we hadn't met before and will likely never meet again. We got introduced to each other and were asked to start off by describing a story about our youth. Interestingly, most of us had similar stories to share about humanity, joy, and compassion. During this program we learnt that in this modern world we have become perpetual footballs of other people's emotions and actions. If somebody is vile towards us, we retaliate either immediately or just hide it and hit back later. We all have forgotten our true human nature.

During the program we also learnt how to breathe in a rhythmic fashion with sequences set out by a facilitator. We performed some simple yoga exercises and ate food that made us feel light and rejuvenated. Every part of the program had been designed to make us feel relaxed and our own Self.

And then came the most powerful thing that I had ever done until then. We sat opposite from each other, held hands, looked into each other's eyes, and said to this stranger, "I belong to you." That was it. My floodgates opened. I just could not hold my tears back. I had not cried after my father's death; not in front of my mother, my spouse, my children, or anyone else. I felt so mesmerized by this stranger's pair of eyes. I felt as if Divinity had descended on earth that day and taken away all my sorrow. Everywhere I looked in the room, everyone had tears of gratitude in his or her eyes. Something moved in us with those four words. I now think of those words every time I get upset at someone and the differences just go away. How powerful.

I had not been to a temple for years on end, but now I wished to learn more about my religion. Where did my forefathers come from? What did Vedanta, the knowledge of the Vedas, provide to us? What are the teachings of the Gita? Are there similarities between the Gita and the Bible and the Quran? I started to read voraciously even though I had a twelve-hour-a-day job, young kids, and a blossoming clinical, teaching, and research career. And you know what – I could still do it. I was blessed to find knowledge everywhere I looked. I started to acknowledge that as a seeker

I would gain the knowledge if I just looked with an open mind. I had to learn how to undo or unravel the complexities of life that were in front of me. I felt so blessed that I wished to write this book. I am eternally grateful to my own guru whose thoughts and teachings continue to inspire and guide me through everything that I do.

Vedanta teaches that everything you see is not real; that the whole world you see is not really true. Vedanta uses the word maya to describe this concept. The word maya is so beautiful as it provides us wonderful insight into so many things in creation. We live in a materialistic world where items are bartered using money, be it dollars or another currency, or now, the growing virtual currencies. If you need something, you need to pay for it with something. This method of exchanging one material item for another is nothing but maya. The whole world works on the blind faith that you can get something with just a piece of plastic, or a piece of paper, or a coin. Maya is the token when our intention is love. We love someone and that is why we want to give someone something. As soon as we give a part of ourselves, we feel the need to receive. This receivership or doership makes us stuck in maya again and we are not able to see the inherent love that started the process of loving, giving, and receiving. Maya is like a Fool's Gold, which keeps us stuck in this world. We need to always remember that we are not the money nor wealth that we inherit or earn. Nor are we the job that we do or the fame that we generate in our job or the respect that we receive. Nor are we the family or relatives that we think define us. We are much more than that. Behind the Fool's Gold are the actual jewels and treasure, which are undetectable by an ignorant eye. Indeed it is a truth that a human being is happier when he has less material wealth. It is also a truth that you can have all the wealth that this world has to offer and still be happy and joyful and enlightened.

Confused?

Indeed maya is just a concept that we are all living in. This whole world is also maya; not just the wealth, but each and every aspect of this creation that our eyes can see and our other sense organs perceive. My thoughts, feelings, emotions, and wealth are limited and all of them are maya, while my true nature is limitless and infinite. I just need to accept this and acknowledge that I am much more than what I see and feel. As you unfold into your true Self, maya slowly disappears. Acknowledging that there is something above and beyond what is visible and perceptible is the first step in accepting that maya is illusionary and helps us get rid of our ignorance. Let us look beyond maya. Let us reflect and contemplate on something that makes us find our own centred, and aware Self.

Beyond maya is the supreme Consciousness or the Divine, which makes everything work.

The great thinkers of the modern world are indeed recognizing that the limits of physics will soon be reached. Stephen Hawking, one of the most respected modern physicists, acknowledges that the concept of what sustains the whole visible and perceptible external world, which is a million million million million meters big (twenty four zeros), and the nano world, which is a millionth of a millionth of a millionth of a millionth meter small, cannot exist by the same principles. There is a sort of energy at the macro and the micro level, which the hadron collider and the Hubble telescopes just cannot explain. At the level of quarks, what is that God principle which keeps it all together? Perhaps we need to learn the principles that control each aspect of this creation.

d) The Vedantic Way of Enlightenment: Dharma, Karma, Prema, Jnana

Vedanta expounds that all things, big and small, have four basic philosophies that govern their functioning.

- Dharma or duty or the natural state of doing things
- Karma or action
- Prema or love
- Jnana or knowledge.

Let me offer my simplistic understanding of this very deep yet basic knowledge. We consider *dharma* as what is appropriate for things/objects/

living organisms to do. Everything has a role. The role of a rock is to sit on the ground and just be there. The role of the grass is to tap into the water and the sun, turn green, and provide a ground for earthworms and other organisms to live in. Similarly all animals have roles to live too, which have been preordained by the Divine. We, as human beings, have been designed to have a much bigger role than others. Indeed we are recognizing that a lot of animals have abundance of intelligence and that they are able to communicate very well with each other, show compassion, reproduce, and perform so many other functions. But it is only man who has been provided a very powerful intellect, which makes him able to understand and differentiate the Real from the Un-Real, the Truth from the False, the Finite from the Infinite. In Sanskrit, this knowledge is called *Viveka* or Knowledge of Discrimination. Of course with our intellect we have been able to make so many advances in science as well, which has led to so much ease and comfort in our daily lives. The trajectory of secular growth has been tremendous over the last few centuries, however, spiritual growth has been a bit slower. It is time for this to move forward too.

To follow our *dharma*, every object and living organism has to do some *karma* or action too. The role of the rock is to indeed sit as it was provided with that ability only. Learned people have learnt so much from rocks as well; we learn how to remain still and unperturbed in the face of adversity. Come what may, rain or shine, light or day, I will continue to find the Divine in everything that I see around me. For human beings, the concept of karma has been very well defined. We will explore this later in another section of the book.

Prema, or love, is the inherent nature of everything in this creation. It is the force that keeps it all together. It is the basic tenets of the infinite Consciousness, which creates, maintains, and destroys everything. It's quality and breadth is more than the love that is in common usage. We understand love as a feeling that we have towards our family or a loved one. That is a very small portion of our infinite potential.

Prema, or the infinite love, permeates everywhere; through time, across all boundaries, and at the macro and micro level. This is the same force that keeps the electrons going around the protons and the neutrons, the planets around the stars, and is behind gravity and the existence of the universe. All learned people describe it as a source of light, which is so bright that it cannot be described. On attainment of liberation, or moksha, it is said that we feel this Love permeate through our every organelle, cell, organ, and part of our bodies and we become one with the Divine. All the religions, spiritual beliefs, scriptures, and learned ones teach us how to find this love by letting go of our egos, loving everything and everyone, doing our karma without any expectations, following our dharma, and remembering the knowledge which is the Ultimate Truth. Let us not forget that we can all get on the path to be liberated. That is our fundamental right, the true freedom that we can all achieve.

Jnana, or knowledge, according to Vedanta, is very straightforward. It is so simple, so potent, and freely available without any cost, yet so priceless. It is a *mahavakya* (great saying) expounded by the sages and is called *Aham Brahmasmi* (I am Brahman or the Divine or the Supreme consciousness).

The Brahman is what is present everywhere and in everything. It is the essence or the nature of everything. It the supreme consciousness that is beyond the concepts of time and space. It is infinitely large, as it encompasses the universe(s), as well as infinitesimally small, as it is the building block of everything. It is the source of life and also the source of destruction. It contains all the emotions, including feelings of sorrow and happiness. It is the substratum on which everything works. This consciousness can be understood as the electricity in the bulb, which helps the bulb light up. If we were to consider our bodies as the wick, the supreme consciousness is what makes our bodies think, feel, breathe, and live.

To keep this world interesting, the Divine also instilled in each of us an ego. The presence of the ego makes us forget our infinite potential. The man of wisdom knows this truth, goes beyond his ego, is therefore able to recognise his full potential, and is thus liberated. You too can reduce your ego to a point where it becomes negligible and your own body, mind, and intellect merge with the super body, mind, and intellect of God's universe. Various practices help us reach our full potential. We will read about these throughout the rest of this book.

Now, thinking of this further logically, if we all have an innate or the supreme consciousness and there is a layer of ego that does not allow us to reach our full potential; then there must perhaps be some further layers that need to be transgressed or traversed through before we can realize our full potential. Various teachers from the past understood that human beings come not only in different shapes and sizes, but have different amount of "impressions" that prevent them from knowing their true nature. These impressions are also called "Vasanas." Let us explore this concept a bit further.

As we perform our karma in this world, our necessary actions, we are in this process laying down new impressions at some level of our consciousness. Our karmas are dictated, at least in the non-enlightened state, by our impressions. Let me give you an example: I happen to enjoy sweets more than savouries, so because of these impressions, which have been laid down in my mind, I will prefer eating a sweet if presented with an option of choosing between a sweet and a savoury. I will continue to lay this same impression again and again until the time I die. When, and if I do get born again (if you accept the concept of reincarnation) I will likely enjoy sweets again without realizing why I prefer them in the next life!

I might also have impressions based on my experiences from earlier on in my life. If I have always felt a bit suspicious of someone, it could be because I have had a past experience of someone taking away something that I wished to have. From then on, I will likely be suspicious of other people's intentions and actions. Modern psychiatry understands this concept more in terms of personality structure, thinking style, cognitive styles, and metacognitions. I think the word "impression" is much simpler because it takes away the onus of one's thinking style and puts it on something, which by definition, is in the past. And as we all know, the past cannot be changed. Most conditions of the mind can be understood as a manifestation of impressions laid down in us. We will discuss this concept further in subsequent sections of the book.

e) The Three Gunas

The teachers from the past also recognized that besides our impressions, we are also subject to some styles of doing things because of three types of inherent "gunas" that we all express, which are needed for us to function as human beings. The extent of the intensity of these three gunas can differ for each and every person and additionally can vary depending on the time of the day.

The three gunas are:

1. Rajas
2. Tamas
3. Sattva

Rajas guna is what provides us with the energy to act. It is a replenisher, makes us do things, gets us out of lethargy, and helps us perform during the day. The *Tamas* guna is the opposite, as it makes us feel tired, depleted, and lethargic. It drains us of our energy and helps us go to sleep. *Sattva* is a state where our minds are completely relaxed and we are full of contentment, yet we are able to think and plan ahead.

All the three gunas are states of mind and are influenced by day-to-day happenings and the time of day, and they result in the mood that we find ourselves in. You would have noticed that there are some people who are the sharpest early during the day; they are full of energy in the morning and able to perform many activities during the early part of the day. However, they succumb to being tired by the evening as their Tamas starts to grow. On the other hand, there are other people who feel more charged up in the evening so their Rajas is higher in the evening, while their Tamas is more pronounced in the mornings.

From the account above, you will be able to appreciate that Sattva is the state that is optimum for our performance. If Rajas is too high we are emotionally charged up and are not able to tap into our full potential. If Tamas is too high, we feel tired and dull. If we were to acknowledge and accept that everything in the world is changing, then by logic alone we would realise that none of these three states are permanent.

The person who is Self-realised watches life, without being affected by these three gunas. He is more than Sattva, as he has transcended even this state. Rather, whatever he does leads to the generation of Sattva for others.

We do know that when we are going through a depressive episode, when everything looks dark and bleak, nothing seems positive, and we are tired and non-interested, that is when the Tamas guna has taken over us. Similarly, a person going through a manic episode does not feel the need to go to sleep, is full of energy, and feels that he can make a difference to the world with his great ideas and inventions. In that person, Rajas is really high.

We also know that nobody can always remain depressed or manic. With or without medication, both these states eventually dissipate. The psychiatrist only tries to manage these mood states with medications by correcting the chemical imbalance that could be causing such mood states. But ask any psychiatrist and he or she will acknowledge that we really do not know what drives a depressive mood or a manic mood. We only broadly know that mood resides in various brain systems and that chemicals like dopamine, norepinephrine, serotonin are likely unbalanced in such depressive or manic states. We do have various medications available that can alter these mood states by selectively influencing some or more of these chemicals and their actions on various receptors. However, the chances of making these mood states go away more quickly are better when the patient expresses faith in the medication and the doctor – faith that he will get better. And that is the healing power of faith. Psychiatry is the only field where placebo responses can be as high as fifty percent in randomized controlled trials. This just again proves the potential of faith in managing various mental health conditions.

Psychiatrists know for sure, though, that when a depressive mood is really bad and dips to a level where nothing seems positive in the world, the whole world seems dangerous. When we are so tired and lethargic that we can stay the whole day in bed, when our appetite becomes rubbish and we lose all hope for the future, then the condition has become really severe. Antidepressants don't really work that well at this point. For some strange reason, the mind literally needs to be shaken out of this type of thinking and feeling.

At the current moment of time, modern science shows that we have two types of treatment that seem to work when one is in such a state of mind: Electroconvulsive therapy (ECT) and Transcranial magnetic stimulation (TMS). Both these types of treatments have response rates of as high as ninety percent compared to fifty percent with antidepressants. How ECT or TMS work is even more poorly understood, compared to the progress in understanding the mechanisms of action in antidepressants. What we do know is that these therapies literally help minds reset into their usual calm states. The tamasic guna is reset so that the mind is able to enjoy some rajas as well as sattvik states.

f) The four S's: Seva, Sadhana, Satsanga, Shraddha

Eons ago, the great sages gave us various techniques to balance these energy states to allow us to go closer to the transcendental state, which crosses these three states. The easiest way to remember them is the four S's.

1. Seva or selfless service
2. Sadhana or various spiritual practices, including yoga-asanas, prayer, meditation, and breathing techniques
3. Satsanga or good company
4. Shraddha or faith in the Divinity

The interesting part is that if we practice these four S's all the time, with complete dedication and discipline, all our lower desires just fall off and we are on the path to enlightenment. We feel more contented, the three gunas do not control our lives, we do not succumb to our desires, and life appears to be a blessing. Let us read more about these techniques so that we can put them into our daily practice.

SEVA

I am sure you must have met someone who works tirelessly for others, but who just does not care about what other people think or about the implications that it might have on his own personal and family life. Have you felt that he /she has an aura around himself/herself. You would have felt relaxed and happy in this person's presence.

The interesting part is that most people do have opportunities to offer selfless service, but they let these opportunities go by. There is always the excuse of time, or commitment to family, or non-availability, physical health issues, mobility problems, or transportation difficulties. Yes, we have heard them all and I have myself resorted to some of these excuses in the past. Now I yearn for an opportunity to serve wherever I can, whoever I can. That is because I know that the reward after completing a volunteering activity is peace, which can last for a really long while. I have now become greedy to offer Seva and now it is in my nature. If I have done a Seva activity on a particular day, my meditation is at a different level and my Sattva levels are much higher. There is something about giving which is wholesome and rewarding.

However, we need to be aware that volunteering and charity have become buzz-words for some people who are trying to make a quick buck as they appeal to people's sensitivities and compassion. This needs to be avoided. We need to utilize our intelligence to differentiate between true volunteering opportunities versus a situation where someone is taking us for a ride.

Some learned teachers have also said that if you work with complete dedication and interest in doing good for humanity, even if you are offered material wealth as a salary or honorarium, you will still receive the rich benefits of Seva. As long as you have the intention to truly help another person then Seva's benefits will be felt by you and your loved ones.

SADHANA

Sadhana is a Sanskrit word that means various spiritual practices. This word is very rich in meaning. Sadly, language can only deliver so much and I might not be able to adequately translate the word. Sanskrit is the language of eons ago, which arose from the people living in the land of the Indus and Ganges. The word Sanskrit also means "refined speech." Sadhana includes various techniques suggested by the sages to accomplish yoga, a word that literally means to join with the eternal. Of course the modern understanding of yoga is simply as yogic exercises of various sorts, but those are just yoga-asanas. Sadhana involves various techniques where yoga occurs. The true meaning of yoga is becoming one with the eternal. This could be possible through appreciating art, playing music, being active in a sport, doing yoga-asanas, performing work with complete dedication, and of course various breathing and meditation techniques.

Have you noticed that when you are completely immersed in work, you feel so relaxed and calm? However, if there are things bothering you, at the back of your mind, your body twitches, you feel pain in various parts of your body, you get irritated by various environmental noise and so you can never achieve perfect Sadhana. Hence, even in the vocational world, the sages have suggested that if you perform work that you are passionate about, you will be joyful.

If we wish to get into a higher level of consciousness for joining ourselves with the Self, we can just let go of our material selves and be in peace with who we are, where ever we are. This can be done through prayer, meditation, or yoga-asanas. The importance of self-discipline and regularity helps us to get the maximum benefit from such techniques. It is well known that the path of spirituality is not a pleasant one, but it is definitely a good one. We will certainly have some days where, try as we may, we feel pulled down by bad thoughts, and our minds will be fickle and not rest on one thought. The Divine, though, has provided an intellect, which we should use to direct our thoughts back to the Divine.

I have not met one person yet who has said that his/her mind is completely calm and composed throughout the whole time, or every time that he/she meditates. I suspect it is only the enlightened souls who can go into a deep stage of meditation very quickly and also put other people in the room into a deep state of relaxation quickly. If you can, find such a person to help you on your journey to spirituality. Hence, the paramount importance of finding a teacher or a guru, to keep you on your spiritual path.

But this book is not about promoting one particular type of Sadhana technique. Whatever works for you is good enough. Try a few and then stick to one. I have met a few people who do a bit of spirituality shopping. They want to try Mindfulness, Transcendental Meditation, Loving-Kindness Meditation, Passionate Meditation, Biofeedback, Hatha yoga, Tai-Chi and more and more but just cannot find one to settle on. This mind, when it is learning to be on the spiritual journey, needs life to be simple so that it can learn and practice such ancient techniques. It gets confused when too many techniques are tried out.

I really liked one abbreviation which one of my patients shared with me: KISS. Keep It Simple Stupid. Do one simple Sadhana technique that you can do daily, which suits your body, mind, and intellect and then observe great things happen.

SATSANGA

The power of humanity lies in the verbal and non-verbal contact that every human being provides. If we are in good company, then the other person's positive thoughts and feelings have a positive effect on us too. Have you not felt that some people radiate a sort of positive energy as soon as they enter into a room? If you have, I can bet you that they also had a lot of positive virtues in them. Positivity exudes outward and cleanses everything in contact with it, whereas negativity sticks like a glue; it tries to keep evil/bad thoughts together.

A man's mind is weak, and inevitably it might be pulled into negative directions by the negative things that he is exposed to. The gossipers and the scaremongers find some level of relief for themselves by letting go of their own anxiety by talking to other people. Staying with them will inevitably make you feel scared and anxious, it is but natural. Similarly, if you were to stay with people who are angry, jealous, vile, anti-social, grandiose, passive-aggressive, narcissistic, or paranoid, they will project these negative feelings on to you and you will get affected. It is but natural too. As you read these above qualities, you might in your mind automatically remember a number of thoughts and feelings you can associate with people in your life who have such propensities.

An enlightened person will not be affected by these feelings because he recognizes that these are devilish thoughts, which are also a manifestation of the Divine. The enlightened person remains calm, composed, and compassionate in whatever comes across his way. In fact, he becomes stronger in the face of the adversity posed by the people with such qualities with whom he comes into contact.

However, you and I are seekers in the initial stages of spirituality and are not as strong yet. As a result, we have to make a constant effort to stay away from people with bad vices. If they do come in contact with us we should try to find the Divinity in them, which has been clouded over by their ignorance. An interesting secret for the seeker is that good people attract good anyway. So you do not need to feel bad that you are letting go of some of your "friends," if you know that they do not have enough virtuous thoughts and feelings. If there is a strong desire and yearning for becoming good, the bad fall off by themselves. They are like dead leaves on our branches of life. The new leaves are brighter and stronger from seeking to capture the strength of the wonderful light and energy of the sun, our Divine keeper.

So don't feel guilty if some of these bad leaves had to fall off. New leaves have to grow. The whole world is only about change, and for us to have a positive change we have to let go of negative thoughts and feelings as well as negative associations.

This world can seem Heaven to people when they see the Divinity everywhere or it can seem like Hell when they only see death, poverty, sickness, drug problems, or corruption. Depends on how we look at it. So let us associate with good people because they are closer to the Divine as the Self is infinite and changeless and it is possible to merge with Him through gratitude and prayer. The bad thoughts will just leave us, as they do not have the power; they are by nature projections of the mind. The truth is hidden. It is a secret, which becomes clearer and clearer as we continue on this journey. Have faith.

SHRADDHA

They say you need to have faith to jump over the last precipice of doubt. By nature, our minds are scared of the unknown. How can I have faith when there is no proof that the Divine exists? I am OK with the way I am living. I am provided for, I have a job, I have a family to look after, so how do you expect me to jump over that precipice?

All the sages from time immemorial have said that you need to take the leap of faith through complete surrender to the Divine. If he has provided for you, then why are you scared that these materialistic things will be taken away if you are to travel the path of the Divine? They have all said that once you have surrendered magical things happen, and what you need, will be provided.

A student never doubts the knowledge that is being provided by his teacher, because he has faith that the english, mathematics and science that he is learning from this teacher are the best. In addition, parents send their children to school because they have faith in the school as well as the teachers. Let us now reflect on who made these parents, teachers, and schools in the first place. There has to be a reason for them being there. Look anywhere and you will realize that each and every system works only on faith. The doctor has faith in his medicine, and the patient has faith in his doctor, so he takes his medications in the faith that he will get better. We have faith in the transport system and thus; we can buy our tickets through a web page, which is located on a server in some part of the world; the payment is processed through an agency, which confirms your tickets; and you have faith in the airport and its staff to take you from point A to B. If there were no faith none of these systems would work. Faith exists because we unknowingly do acknowledge the role of the Divine in everything. Now all you need to do is completely surrender to the infinite. Any act that you do is going to be for the general good for you, your loved ones, and society. Because, remember, you are Divine.

Let me share with you one story of faith that I often heard as a young child in India. This is the story of Ekalavya, a character from the Hindu epic Mahābhārata.

Ekalavya wished to learn archery. However, he was the son of a poor hunter who could not afford for his son to be taught by a teacher trained in the science; a guru. Nevertheless, Ekalavya took it upon himself to find a guru who could teach him, and he chose the best of the best. He went to Dronacharya, considered a master of advanced military arts, and requested him to teach him archery. But Dronacharya did not accept Ekalavya as his pupil because he had a conflict. He was the teacher for the sons of the royal family and as such he could not teach the son of a hunter.

In those days in India, if you were a teacher of the royal princes, then you could not accept anyone else as your pupil. Any act that could make another equal in ability and prowess to the princes, would be considered sacrilege. The kingdom would no longer be safe or secure.

Even so, Ekalavya considered Dronacharya to be his guru in principle. He went home and made a statue of Dronacharya and learnt archery from the statue. It was as if Dronacharya were giving him instructions through the insentient rock. The power of the guru was so strong that Ekalavya's abilities grew to the point that he became even better than the best of Dronacharya's disciples, Prince Arjuna.

One day, Prince Arjuna found out about Eklaya's abilities. He saw that Ekalavya was far more skilled than he. So he went to Ekalavya and asked him, "Who is your guru?"

Ekalavya said, "Dronacharya is my guru."

Upset, Arjuna then went back to Dronacharya and started to shout at him, "What is this? This is cheating. You were supposed to teach only me, but you taught this boy as well and made him more skilful than me."

Dronacharya was baffled. He knew he had not taught anyone except the royal princes. Dronacharya and Arjuna then went together to meet this boy, to try to understand how he had learnt to be an expert archer without having the guru teach him. Ekalavya led them to the statue that he had made of Dronacharya, which he considered as his guru.

On seeing this, Dronacharya said, "Now you have to give me some guru-dakshina," (a gift as fees for learning). He asked Ekalavya to give him the thumb of his right hand as a gift. Ekalavya knew that without his right thumb he would no longer be an archer. Still, he did not think twice. He cut off his thumb and offered it in complete faith, obedience, and respect to his guru.

One way to interpret this story is that Dronacharya was cruel, because he robbed the student of his skill. But if we examine this story critically, were it not for this incident, history would not have been written about Ekalavya. Though superficially it seems as if Dronacharya had done injus-tice to Ekalavya, it is likely that Dronacharya uplifted Ekalavya, because this one act made him immortal and we are still reading this story. There could not be a better story about devotion and faith, and everyone remem-bers Ekalavya, not Arjuna, who though he had the same guru, was only able to become the best because Ekalavya was taken out of the equation.

We can also appreciate the greatness of Dronacharya, the guru, as he took the blame for having taught Ekalavya even though he never physically taught Ekalavya. Through his request to Ekalavya to give up his thumb, he lifted Ekalavya to a level where we respect him to the point of rever-ence. It is therefore said that even if the guru appears to be wrong, if you have full faith in the guru, you can never ever go wrong. The rever-ence that Ekalavya displayed towards his guru is worthy of emulating. An unquestioning faith in the teacher leads to extraordinary teaching. This story also shows that the guru managed to preserve his dharma (duty) of being a teacher to the Royal family only.

g) Love, Prayer, and Forgiveness

LOVE

One common thread of discussion that I see for myself as well as for other families is the need to love and be loved. As human beings, we go through a beautiful phenomenon called "falling in love." Sounds strange, doesn't it? As if we have to stoop or fall backwards to be in love. The person who is deeply in love, knows how much higher one feels when in that feeling. Nothing seems to be as important as being with the close one. There is a yearning from the heart to associate with, to be with, and to become one with the other person. It is such an inexplicable phenomenon that books, movies, and TV try to capture this for us in story after story. But do such stories always have a happy ending?

No. Inevitably one person starts to "fall out of love," as if we had fallen once and we fall again.

The beauty of the skin, the glance from the eyes, the smile, the expression of the eyes, can literally attract one person to another to such an extent that the person stops thinking. We become completely entwined in this feeling. Intellect goes to the bin and we feel so joyous. However, this form of love can turn into greed too – greed to receive from and become a part of the other. The seers describe this feeling of love as lust. Lust for the body. When we get it once, we want it more and more. And when we do not receive it enough, we feel really hurt. And then we become angry and upset.

The seers describe several other forms of love. There's also the love that we associate with just being with the loved one, or a pet, a wonderful work of art, soulful music, and so on. Vedanta calls this love the Supreme Consciousness. It permeates through everything at a macrocosmic, as well at a microcosmic level.

Can we understand this love using modern science? Perhaps we will in the future but not yet. Even with modern advances we are really not able to understand why gravitational force really exists. Why is there dark matter or dark energy? Why do various cells in our bodies stay together? We can therefore conceptualise that there is some sort of an energy that keeps everything together. What we know is that the cells are together and that is it – the bottom line. So let us accept it and hence call it love.

At the emotional level, let us consider anger and greed as nothing but expressions of love. It is because we love someone that we express our anger towards him or her. If we did not love someone that much we would not care to express our anger, would we? Anger is just upside-down love. Greed is nothing but loving objects more than life. We become attracted to these objects and cannot but express greed when somebody else has an object we desire.

So if love is the basis of this creation, why do I need to fret when I do not receive enough or receive it in a lopsided way? The very fact that I am alive and am a storehouse of love received and sent is such a powerful thought. The Creator loves each and every morsel and particle with which He filled me with love. So let me just revel in this knowledge and life will seem so much calmer and more blissful. If we accept the fact that our innate nature is love, then we will feel so at ease. We will find no physical or emotional difference between ourselves and the people to whom we wish to show our love. Of course, it is up to these people to accept our love. If they do not wish to be part of the love circle, well it is their problem and we need to move on. If our love is genuine and from the heart, then we are pure. That is what matters. We have surrendered ourselves. So don't be grumpy or upset if somebody does not love you back.

Another important factor to consider is that love changes over a period of time. Remember who you were at the time that you had your first crush and the person you are now; they are so different. If time changes so many things, will love for one person not change too? The quality, the texture of love in a married couple who have been together for twenty years or more is very different from that of those who have recently gotten married. If the love that you are showing towards your loved one is only for giving rather for than the expectation of receiving anything, then your love will flourish. Any expectation from a loved one leads to a rise of the ego as a barrier and the love may flounder. You will then have negative thoughts of anger, jealousy, suspicion, and paranoia. Stop yourself from reacting when you hear some negative comment from a loved one. You react because your ego is hurt and you feel the need to retaliate. Immediately laugh at the emotions arising in you at that time. That is the only way. If you try to rationalize or make sense of why you are reacting, you have already lost the battle. Remember love and ego are not rational. They are just phenomena. And love is infinite. So how can we try to define an infinite thing?

Inevitably if something as infinite as love exists, it cannot be that simple to understand and appreciate. There will be layers of knowledge to be transcended to really understand love. Ego is nothing but such a layer and it was made by the Divine to help us differentiate our own physical bodies from each other's; to recognize duality. But our intellect knows that everything is one. Ego is nothing but a phenomenon in this wonderful creation. Acknowledge it, accept it, laugh at it, and move on. Love shall then blossom. And you will be like a child giggling away in merriment and laughter at every thing you see. Consider this knowledge when you interact with a person with whom you are not getting along too well and laugh out loud every time you feel upset for whatever reason.

The whole of this creation is full of love. Not even one inch is without love. You can tap into this energy of love. It is fathomless and it is your nature. Love, when applied with this wisdom, turns into eternal bliss. We have learnt from this wisdom that there is no duality in this world. Everything is one. You do not see a difference between you and the other person. This thought will allow you to love each and everyone and the creation. So just give. Do not expect. That is it. The next time that I feel that someone does not love me, I just need to say to myself that I am a Divine person who is full of love. Let me give my love to everything and everyone.

PRAYER

There is a reason for the emphasis on praying in most religions and spiritual belief systems. There are innumerable stories of miracles happening with prayers alone. Most learned people acknowledge the power of prayer as it helps the person find his connection with the inner Self. Spiritually it makes so much sense to go into a deeper connection with the Creator through simple requests and prayers.

The more I read about various religions, the more I realize how powerful prayers can be. There are innumerable tales of the power of prayer. Just wishing something positive for someone could lead to that happening. Sometimes, when I see that my medications or the psychotherapy that I offer are not working, I silently pray for the person. I do this quietly without mentioning it to any one. Lo behold, my patients soon feel relieved. The severity of their depressive symptoms or their psychosis or the extent of their alcohol or other addictions, or the severity of their anxiety have magically improved without any major intervention from me.

A person who prays regularly is tapping into the infinite potential of the Divine. He is there to help because he knows that there is suffering in this world. If there was no suffering we would not appreciate the positive aspects of the world. We appreciate goodness only when we can compare it with badness or wickedness in someone else. We appreciate somebody's good physical health only if we notice that somebody else is riddled with cancer or suffering from a mental illness.

However, do not expect that all prayers will be answered. That would be disrespectful of an important concept of this creation. The value of prayer is best understood with the Vedantic concept of Viveka, or wisdom; knowing that this whole world is changing on a substratum of that which is not changing. As a seeker I need to constantly appreciate that this mind and body are incessantly changing. What I see, feel, and hear are continuously changing, and then there is something that I am comparing it with. It is the Self, which does not change at all. Identify yourself with that part of you, everywhere you place your sight, hearing, or touch. Feel the duality merge into singular truth. Love becomes your very nature when you live this truth. The power of your prayer grows.

But never take pride in your ability to make a positive impact on someone with your prayer. If in your spiritual practices you see that you can make people better and you start to have a feeling of pride, then your ability to heal will recede. Anybody can heal as long as he or she does not wear the clothes of pride. Let us be our true nature; pure, untouched, and loving towards everybody and everything in this creation.

Let not any vice touch your heart. May you live long to work ceaselessly for others. May you find strength in any situation, may you never feel despondent or miserable, whatever the circumstances in which you find yourself. May you remain healthy and provide succour to those who need your help in their illness. I pray for you.

FORGIVENESS

To forgive others, first we need to forgive ourselves. This is an innate requirement for someone on the spiritual path. The ever loving Self, the Divine, by nature is infinite and has produced this creation for the enjoyment of everyone. As long as one stays on the path of virtue, one will continue to grow on a spiritual basis. If we do make mistakes, all we need to do is ask forgiveness for ourselves. As we walk on the spiritual path, our faith in the concept of forgiveness grows and we are able to forgive others, including our loved ones. What continues to help me keep my faith in humanity is this very concept of forgiveness. We hear so many stories that when one forgives the other, he or she becomes so much stronger. The more that we are able to embrace our adversary, the lighter we feel in our spirit and calmer in our selves.

Here is a real-life story. Early one morning, Matt Swatzell, a firefighter, was driving home from a twenty-four-hour shift after having slept only thirty minutes. He suddenly heard a crashing sound. Matt realized he had fallen asleep at the wheel and had had an accident. When he got out, he saw he had crashed into the car of a young woman, June Fitzgerald. She was clearly pregnant and was with her then nineteen-month-old daughter Faith. Faith survived the crash but her mother and her unborn child died in the accident.

June's husband, Erik Fitzgerald, was a full-time pastor, and understandably was extremely grieved by the loss of his wife and unborn child. One young girl from his ministry went up to him and said she couldn't help but think of how the driver of the car was feeling after the accident. I found this part of the story most poignant.

A thought that I wish us to ponder and reflect upon: isn't it so interesting that young children have nothing but pure consciousness flowing through them? The young girl thought first about the person who was left behind. She could empathise with the guilt flowing through the mind of the driver of the car. Her first thoughts were not for the person who was already dead. Killing someone accidently is not a crime in the eyes of the law, but it does leave one terribly wounded in the soul. Having compassion for such a person, caring for them, or being with them is our dharma.

Without letting his ego, or his sense of anger and retribution take control of him, Erik listened to this young person. He told her that she was right, and that they should all pray for Matt Swatzell. It was his opportunity to practice the forgiveness he had preached so many times before. "You forgive as you've been forgiven," said Fitzgerald.

Fitzgerald's forgiveness has since created a friendship, which has remained wonderfully strong. Erik and Matt have stayed connected by meeting at least once every two weeks, attending church together, and eating meals at the Waffle House and other restaurants. Their friendship was captured in a video produced by NewSpring Church, which was shot in 2011 and has been seen by hundreds of thousands of people.

From potential enemies to life-long friends – this story really moved my heart and I hope it moves yours too.

As a person living in this materialistic world of ours, of course, one might sometimes question what the point is of forgiveness when the ones who are corrupt do "make it to the top" and oppress others during the process. So a thought process for us could be: *I can be a little bit deceitful, get what I need, and everything will be just fine. I know I am not hurting anyone.* These are common defensive thoughts whenever we commit a crime, small or big. We have let such thoughts come into our minds, inevitably, because of our own personal experiences as well as the observations, stories, and events that have made us question the very nature of humanity and society. We see corruption rampant everywhere, feel sorry for the people who have to go through it, and feel sad when we come across a person affected by it.

Isn't it time we awoke and took some action against corruption rather than being mute spectators? Let us begin the process from inward to make us stronger so we can fight corruption.

During our lives we will continually come across situations where we have to choose the **right** path, the one which we know is correct. Our gut tells us that this is the right way, not another one that might look easier but has some amount of deceit and corruption and subsequent guilt; the **pleasant** path. It is up to us to choose between these two paths.

Often we choose the pleasant. Who wants to stick to the truly lofty values when we know that the people who chose the right path are not going to do well in the long term? Take Mahatma Gandhi for example. Even though he was the most virtuous, someone chose to shoot him to death. This is just one example of our intellectual defence mechanisms.

Here is a suggestion to help you stay on the right path: As soon as your gut tells you that you have done something wrong, immediately listen to that inner voice and seek forgiveness from yourself and the person that you have hurt. Do not wait for your special prayer time or another day to seek forgiveness. You don't have to go to church, temple, or mosque or find a special moment to ask for forgiveness. If you ask for forgiveness you will not accumulate any bad karma. This is a given. This has been proven again and again. The ever-loving Creator is in you and is helping you grow. He does not judge. He does not need to judge. Everyone has been created by Him. So if you are accepting of your mistake and make efforts to change your ways, He has already forgiven you. Be assured in this knowledge and move on. You will feel so much stronger and more joyful when you make this decision. Your previous misdemeanour will seem so small and pale in comparison with the good that you are now going to do. Just revel in that thought.

And to make you feel a little bit lighter. Here is a joke:

I asked God for a bike but I know God doesn't work that way. So I stole a Harley Davidson instead and asked God for forgiveness!

h) Spiritual Practices: Yoga and Kriya

Hundreds of enlightened sages (also called gurus) over at least the last 7000 years have shown that the principles of Vedanta, and the deep knowledge that they possess, can be extracted and put into daily practice by using simple techniques. I will attempt to describe some of these very briefly. I have refrained from going into too much detail in this book as it has been designed to be just a taste of Vedantic science and knowledge rather than a dissertation. We are indeed all blessed to be currently living in a brave new world where such techniques are much more easily available than they were just a couple of hundred years ago. Previously, gurus dedicated their lives to improving the skills of princes and taught such techniques only to the royal families. Knowledge of such techniques was passed on from one guru to a student (shishya) through ceremonies and sacred rites only. We now live in times where, for the betterment of society, some enlightened sages have brought these techniques across the East and the West. Blessed are we that we can be in touch and learn from such enlightened teachers and their knowledge is available to all of us.

A word of caution, though: There will always be the person masquerading to be a guru, whose retinue could be reasonably big, but when you delve into the knowledge that this person is trying to provide, you find it without the needed depth or even useless and that perhaps there's guile at work. My suggestion to the reader is to listen to your intuition. If you feel that you have found the right guru, you have found him/her. Your intuition will never be wrong. Avoid the rest.

YOGA

The actual meaning of the word yoga in Sanskrit, as we read before, means joining of the body-mind-intellect with our Consciousness, the Atman or the Self. In other words, our whole body-mind-intellect equipment becomes rooted in the Self all the time. The Self is nothing but joy and calmness. So if we practice yoga we will turn into a yogi and we will find enlightenment.

Compare this with what the common language usage of yoga has now become. Yoga is not just about positioning our bodies to get some exercise. That is properly labelled as yoga-asana. (Asana means positions.) Any well-trained yoga teacher, who has been through a few years of training, knows that yoga-asanas are extremely powerful and that just by doing these well, a seeker can become enlightened. For we who are seekers of the art of yoga, just performing the asanas on a regular basis can help settle the body, mind, and intellect and lead to reductions in levels of stress. All good yoga teachers emphasise the need to keep an eye on the breath while completing the asanas. If the inhalation and exhalation patterns are done wrongly or if we apply too much effort to get into a position, then we could cause ourselves more harm than good.

Though it is such a good thing that this ancient science of yoga is now more freely available across the world, I really fret when I hear about so many yoga studios that are marketing yoga, who do not understand, appreciate, or care about the knowledge behind this ancient science and apply it wrongly. Yoga is not about heating up your body in extremely humid conditions, forcing yourself to sweat to lose weight, or to get toned up, or to do manoeuvres. It is more about respecting your body and letting it get into a comfortable position and then pressing it just a teeny-weeny little bit more, but never too much.

From my own personal experience, I note that it is now so much easier for me to get into a yoga-asana compared to when I started practicing yoga just a few years ago. I am sure that during this time it has been my mind that has undergone a change, not my body. I know I am now middle-aged, so clearly my body could not have become more flexible. That sounds logically impossible. It is my mind that has become more sensitive and accommodating as well as sharp, which has convinced my body that I can get into these poses more easily.

One of my yoga masters shared his knowledge that it is actually the mind that prevents you from getting into a particular position – it is never the body. We think that we cannot get into a particular pose because of pain or discomfort. We feel the discomfort a little bit when we get into the position and then we hold ourselves from trying the full position. What we need to do is just continue to breathe normally, focusing our mind on the breath rather than the pain...just push ourselves just a little bit more... and then smile. And lo and behold, you will be bending your back more and you will not be breathless or in distress. What a wonderful nature has our mind.

The benefits of yoga-asanas have been shown to be truly amazing on various body systems, including offering mental and physical health benefits. The benefits of this therapy have been known for years. However, it is only in the last five to ten years that the world has started to research the evidence of these therapies a bit more, using the gold-standard research called the randomized controlled trial. Some researchers have been able to collate and scientifically analyse the overall effects of such a therapy by using systematic reviews to draw conclusions on the safety and effectiveness of a particular treatment. All the results from the randomized controlled trials are put together to estimate the odds of the benefits of the assessed treatment compared to a control, which could either be no treatment or a dummy pill called a placebo.

One recent systematic review entitled "Hatha yoga and Executive Function: A Systematic Review," authored by Luu K and Hall PA in the *Journal of Alternative and Complementary Medicine* in 2015 concluded that hatha yoga shows promise for improving executive function. The term "executive function" is psychological parlance for our brain's ability, which, broadly speaking, helps us to plan activities and engage in simple reasoning. It is essentially a brain function that makes us different from other animals.

The authors reviewed all published randomized controlled studies conducted in healthy adults, children, adolescents, healthy older adults, impulsive prisoners, and medical populations (with the exception of sufferers of multiple sclerosis). The authors found that though the randomized controlled studies are limited in number, their findings consistently show that across these diverse populations, there are better ratios of hatha yoga's benefits compared to a control. They end their report by suggesting that to build on this evidence base further, more good-quality studies are needed that evaluate the efficacy of hatha yoga's effects on executive function.

This is just one report that I refer to. As modern science further explores the benefits of ancient techniques like yoga (and meditation, described later), it is not difficult to predict that the next generation of science and humanity will critically analyse such reports. If the benefits are indeed found to be true, based on these we might considering putting such therapies into common practice across all health sciences.

Vedanta says that practicing any of the following four yogas sincerely can help us attain a higher state of consciousness and enlightenment:

Jnana yoga: Jnana yoga is the path of gaining knowledge from scriptural studies, and the application of this knowledge to enhance our wisdom by reflecting on it through regular introspection and contemplation. It involves deep exploration of the Self by systematically exploring and differentiating the Real from the Unreal. Each religion has its own scriptures and a thorough understanding of this scriptural knowledge with adequate application of it can enlighten a seeker.

Bhakti yoga: Bhakti yoga is the path of devotion, love, compassion, and service to the Divine, which is present in the Self as well as others. All actions are done in the context of remembering the Divine in every activity.

Karma yoga: Karma yoga is the path of action, doing our service without any expectation of fruits arising from it, remaining rooted to our true nature while performing our activities and not letting our egos decide what is the best for us. Everything has to be done selflessly thinking only of others and for the improvement of the needs of the family, the community, country, society, humanity, and creation. As the person who follows karma yoga becomes more established and his ego is washed away, he changes from initially thinking about his own needs to thinking of the needs of creation. It is a fact that we all have to do karma yoga as human beings as it is our natural disposition to act. Even meditating is an act! Hence karma yoga is described by Lord Krishna as the easiest way to achieve enlightenment, especially for one who is of working age and in a job. We explore a bit more of this concept later.

Raja yoga: Raja yoga is a comprehensive method that emphasizes meditation and encompasses the other three types of yoga. It directly deals with the encountering and transcending thoughts of the mind. Hence kriya and meditative practices will fall in this category.

The great sages have said that practicing any one or more of these types of yoga can enlighten a seeker. As long as the seeker is sincere in his practices, and with the grace of the Divine, the seeker continues to achieve higher states of consciousness.

Each human being has a different type of personality, based on his or her predisposition as decided by our gunas (as described previously). Therefore, one can choose to focus on one type of yoga based on one's guna, which is based on one's personality style.

And lastly, to share one more story of a personal nature, I know that I have an intellectual and analytical predisposition. I was aware of this from the time that I was a young kid. The fact that I was able to acquire the education to become a physician speaks to the intellectual inclination. All my colleagues, team members, and likely my patients are aware that I can share evidence-based knowledge of medicines and their role in mental health much more comfortably than engaging in the action-based work of a surgeon. I was, and am still, far more at ease analysing why a particular thing might work in a certain way. I get very interested in research and any new finding I come across needs to be understood, analysed, and broken down for me to accept that it can indeed be brought into regular practice. Just knowing makes me feel so calm and collected. However, a transformation has occurred over the last few months. My bhakti yoga has steadily become very rooted in my personality. I can listen to devotional songs and prayers for hours, and I find complete calmness through these practices. I have become more interested in trying out various musical instruments and experimenting with listening to different types of music. This often raises eyebrows in the car! Anyway, the point is that one's personality can change over a period of time too. Spirituality changes you in so many helpful ways.

I posted the following Facebook comment recently on the personal benefits of spirituality, which I have noticed in myself.

1. You don't need to wait for a period of joy; life seems to be so much more enjoyable even in the most ridiculous situations.
2. You are revved up and feel light at the same time.
3. You are able to ignore other people's shortcomings much more easily and are happier just observing.
4. Work seems so much lighter and the day goes by quickly.
5. You can laugh or smile more easily and sometimes for no obvious reason.

If a couple of years of spiritual seeking, through various aspects of yoga being applied to daily life have led to so many changes in me, I do hope that with His Grace, more positive things will continue to happen and I will be able to let go of my ego more easily. I also pray for you that you remain rooted in your own Self and notice life become much more meaningful. If you have the Grace and you are sincere, you might even find enlightenment.

KRIYA

Amongst the various raj yogas, at least from my own personal experience, I have found kriya the most effective and quickest way of rooting myself to my Self, feeling relaxed and energized within a few minutes of the practice.

Let me start off by describing the physiological basis of the breath and its relationship with the psyche. Isn't it a fact that we all need to breathe to live? As we know, a breath consists of inhalation and exhalation. Each inhalation leads to life-giving oxygen getting into the bloodstream, and each exhalation means discharge of various excretory gases such as carbon dioxide, which is a by-product of the body's metabolism.

Now let's examine the process of breathing psychologically. Have you noticed that when we are anxious, worried, or fearful our breath is fast as well as shallow? We literally hunger for oxygen so that the heart can pump it to the organs that need it the most, such as the brain and the muscles. This is frequently described to anyone with anxiety disorders as the "fight or flight" response. The body is hardwired to this response as it is a basic "animal" tendency in the face of adversity. The person with anxiety disorder has also heard from a psychiatrist or mental health worker that this fight or flight response cannot continue forever as it is physiologically impossible to maintain such a rate of breathing. Imagine yourself feeling panicky all the time for no obvious reason. Most people who experience panic attacks suffer when their anxiety shoots up through the roof, but they are able to stop having these feelings within few minutes. However, people with panic disorder may continue to feel tense, with tightness in their muscles. The person with an anxiety disorder learns behavioural therapies for management of the disorder. Deep, forceful, and slow breathing as well as progressive muscle relaxation are common forms of treatment. Research evidence suggests that these therapies help the person's body relax and that as a by-product, the mind also relaxes. Unfortunately, not everyone finds these techniques very effective and newer treatment options are still needed.

On the other hand, we do know that when we are relaxed or feeling joyful our breath is long and deep. So it is likely, by simple logic, that no one wishes to be anxious or worried, and thus the long, relaxed, deep breath is the natural state of our breathing. Although, it could be that in our busy, stressful lives, we become more prone to use the short, tense breaths instead of the long joyful ones. Hence our bodies become tense and even our voluntary muscles feel pain. It is not uncommon for the anxious person to report tension headaches, because of over-usage of the frontalis muscle in the front part of the head; back pain, because of spasms in the paraspinal muscles in the back; and bruxism, caused by spasms of the masseter muscles in the jaw. Research techniques like electromyography biofeedback show that these selective muscles can be relaxed and their pain can be alleviated.

Now imagine yourself able to breathe in a more relaxed way, allowing all of your muscles to relax and all tension-type headaches to disappear. Over thousands of years, learned masters have shown the benefit of various sequences of breathing exercises, to allow the seeker to go into a deep state of relaxation or meditation. However, this knowledge was kept a secret. In the past, gurus would teach such techniques only to the sincere seeker who was interested in evolving to a higher spiritual level. This was only if the master felt that seeker was ready and able to learn such a technique and then pass it on to another capable student.

Now, in this modern, secular world where there is a very strong need for Vedantic spiritualistic techniques to help society de-stress, some enlightened masters have opened the floodgates and are offering their knowledge to each and every one who is interested. Modern accounts of kriya techniques as taught by the great masters of the recent past include Mahavatar Babaji, Lahiri Mahasaya, Paramahansa Yogananda, and Sri Sri Ravi Shankar. They all likely had somewhat similar techniques with subtle differences in the way it was taught.

We are blessed to be living in these modern times where there is an interest in learning not only from the frontiers of science but also through incorporating knowledge from the past. Research is growing on a particular technique called sudarshan kriya yoga (SKY), taught for more than thirty-five years by the spiritual leader and founder of the Art of Living Foundation, Sri Sri Ravi Shankar. The foundation has more than 15,000 trained teachers who offer courses on SKY all over the world. Most people who have heard of sudarshan kriya yoga just call it the kriya or the breath technique. In brief, sudarshan kriya yoga consists of a prescribed sequence of breathing techniques including pranayama (or the breath which allows life- giving energy into the body), and bhastrika (or the bellows breath) among others. These are coupled with the imparting of knowledge designed to enhance our social/emotional learning skills.

Current science is pointing to the benefits of sudarshan kriya yoga across a wide range of physical and mental health conditions associated with stress. These include beneficial effects on hypertension, diabetes, serum cortisol levels, anxiety disorders, impulsive behaviours, depression, and post-traumatic stress disorder. This suggests that this breathing technique is holistic and likely has effects across multiple organ systems.

i) Dispassion

Let me share with you another story. I just returned from a dinner party last night. It was the usual affair; work colleagues sitting together, talking about various work-related issues intermingled with stories of their personal lives. I got interested in some of the stories because they resonated with my own personal experiences. I shared a story or two, which echoed someone else's, and at other times I remained quiet out of courtesy to the person who was talking and because I didn't have much to say. We ended the evening with everyone going back to their homes and families with some sort of sense of kinship in their guts. But somehow, there wasn't a sense of accomplishment, joy, or complete relaxation – as if we could all have done better in communicating.

Isn't this experience of mine somewhat similar to what you might have had in your interactions at work or at parties or other social gatherings?

The mind is indeed very fickle; it is like the waves of the ocean, which rise and fall. We are tuning into other people's minds when they are sharing their stories. We want to reciprocate as we think that our stories will be similar to theirs; as if our waves are similar to their waves and we mingle. We also want ourselves to feel validated as well as wanted. This phenomenon is nothing but our egos saying, "Hey, listen to me, I have a better story to tell." We let our egos win. We sometimes butt in to tell our stories, and it happens so subtly that no one even realizes it. But that the ego has won leads you to feel somewhat incomplete, and therefore you don't necessarily have a sense of joy or relaxation as you return home.

The beauty of spirituality is that you become much more sensitive to how your own mind and ego work. Dispassion, if and when we were to achieve it fully, would mean a complete relaxation of the mind, in whatever situation, where we would observe each and every situation that we encounter with a complete sense of egoless observation. If and when we were to achieve dispassion we would just laugh at how each person was sharing his or her own story and how it was indeed resonating with ours, while being constantly aware of our own thoughts, feelings, and the ego. We would not be bending into the demands of our egos.

Just watching the marvel of this creation at every moment in our lives is pure dispassion. As soon as we realize that we are more than empty conversations, one-upmanship, subtle bitching, stabbing in the back, or looking for some juicy news so that we can use it to advance our own careers etc. etc., we are letting go of our egos. Try this next time you are at a party. Listen, watch, look but do not react or respond. Marvel at how much people talk. React less and respond minimally. Respect silence. Just be thankful for the opportunity to be in the presence of a colleague. Share information for the betterment of the colleague. Think not about yourself but always the improvement of society in general. Dispassion will grow and you will feel much more relaxed at the end of the evening.

It is said that dispassion is one of the major building blocks for one on the spiritual journey. Some people get scared by the use of this word. They fear that if they are dispassionate, it means they will not be able to enjoy life, that they will become recluses, looked down on by other people in conversations. They worry that they might not fit in well. These thoughts are nothing but our egos speaking in rebellion whenever we wish to be more sensitive. People who are more advanced on their spiritual journeys become much more in tune with their true natures of feeling relaxed and joyful. They are able to watch the playful act of their egos all the time. They actually laugh at their egos, watch how other people's egos are reacting, and enjoy the show. After all, isn't life nothing but an act, a big theatre where many people are talking and trying to make an impression?

Let us watch this wonderful drama with the keen eye of observation, rather than being attached. And let us constantly feel in a state of thankfulness and gratitude to be allowed to be spectators. As we then let go of our egos, we feel less tense and start to smile. We join in much more and enjoy this "leela," or drama, of the Lord. The word "leela" has such a deep meaning, doesn't it?

j) Closing Story

Towards the end of this chapter, I do wish to share another story. I can only apologize in advance if somebody's sensitivity is shaken by it. My intention is not to be a sensationalist but rather to help us contemplate the truth of our living lives. Sadly, a psychiatrist comes across such situations at least a few times in his or her professional life.

It was certainly a very interesting phase in my life, when I faced this situation. It also helped me reflect on the fact that life is actually there to help us understand and appreciate the reason we are alive.

A geriatrician in our acute hospital asked me to take on the care of an elderly woman. The story was strange compared to the usual. This lady, let us call her Nora, had come to the hospital so that the physicians there could help her kill herself. This was the only presenting information. For your knowledge, as of yet, Ontario, Canada, does not legally allow euthanasia.

The geriatrician tried his best to understand why she would wish for that to happen. She looked reasonably healthy; the only physical condition that he could ascertain was a history of diabetes, which in the long run had caused some diabetic neuropathy in her legs. She complained of some tingling and painful sensations in them. However, there was no perceptible difficulty in her motor capabilities and she was able to walk appropriately.

Nora remained adamant that she would not take any pills whatsoever. The social worker tried to contact the family to get some collateral information.

The only person available in the city was a friend, who mentioned that Nora had been living in her basement for the last little while. The friend confirmed that over the last few months Nora had slowly started to give up on her life. She had literally stopped going out of the house. She would remain remorseful, didn't talk much, and had given up on life so much that her personal hygiene had suffered. She was living surrounded by filth and her faeces. Her friend was worried about her, but strangely accepting of Nora's decision to wither away and she was also asking all the physicians to provide euthanasia. It was as if these two women had made a pact that Nora needed to die and that no one in the world could or should save her.

My first few days of trying to know Nora to assess if she was clinically depressed ended up with not much success. She would shout out loud, accusing staff trying to hurt her when they tried to examine her edematous legs. Both of her legs were covered in dry skin, which was a couple of centimetres thick. She would not get up from her bed. She would not eat anything. She wished to only drink ginger ale. She would ask the staff to bring it for her and if they were a few minutes late, she lashed out with the choicest abuses. Our nursing and social work staff is very well trained to assess and help people who have lost touch with reality. Even so, they had no joy in trying to talk to her either. For days on end this continued and Nora was literally dying in front of my eyes. I would come back home every day thinking, *Why is this woman so interested in taking her own life? How can I help her?*

We were later able to make contact with a cousin of Nora's in the United States, who agreed to be the substitute decision maker. She and I agreed that Nora was likely suffering from severe depression, as confirmed by the classical symptoms that one would associate with this illness. These included irritability of mood, paranoid beliefs that people were trying to harm her, profound reduction in appetite, disturbed sleep, lack of energy in the absence of another physical illness, and suicidal presentation. Unfortunately, Nora still would not speak to us, so we really did not know what was going on in her mind. I consulted three of my other colleagues and they all agreed that she had this diagnosis and agreed to a management plan. As she was refusing to take any medications, it was decided to pursue the option of trying out what we know works best in severe depressive psychosis; electroconvulsive therapy (ECT).

I am aware that some of the readers of this book might even fear ECT as it is not very commonly used, there is a lot of bad press around it and there are stories of people losing part of their memories and so on and so forth. But the science and practice of ECT has substantially changed in the last forty-odd years. It is the most researched and evidence-based treatment of severe depression and its response rates are as high as ninety percent compared to around fifty percent for medications and psychotherapies. Additionally, Nora was refusing to take any oral antidepressants or to accept any psychotherapy and she was literally dying in front of our eyes. ECT was the only life-saving treatment available.

After coming to an understanding and appreciation of the risks and benefits of this ECT, Nora's cousin gave us substitute consent to start the treatment. Nora continued to refuse our help and was very upset at receiving this therapy. But although she was unhappy about it, she didn't make a fuss about going off to sleep with the anaesthesia needed prior to each ECT session. As usual, each session lasted only a few seconds under the effects of general anaesthesia and muscle relaxants. After the treatments Nora would keep her eyes closed and still not talk to us except if we wished to examine her legs. She would then shout out and ask us to leave.

I could not elicit the evidence of any memory disturbances with the limited verbal output that Nora had. To remain on the safe side, we chose a modality of ECT where response might be a bit slower but the extent of amnesia (loss in memory) was expected to be minimal. Most patients respond to ECT within five to six sessions, however, Nora continued not to have any response to this form of treatment even after eight sessions. We then had to make the decision for starting some parenteral nutrition to make sure that she did not get dehydrated or have a metabolic imbalance. Nora started to bring up bile repeatedly and continued not to eat or drink anything. This suggested to us that things were not looking good. I gave frequent updates to her cousin and let her know that Nora was literally slipping away.

Just a few days ago Nora passed away. For the first time in the last eight weeks of trying to help her, I felt relieved, not only for my team and myself but for her and her family. It was an ordeal for everyone. It was now over.

It was as if the Divine had agreed with Nora's wishes that she should not be on this planet any more. The very foundation of why a doctor should help a patient was put to question in my mind.

Most professional, religious, and spiritual organizations will not accept suicide as morally or ethically right. And having worked with her as her physician, Nora committed suicide, at least in my eyes. Still, there could be so many other truths in this story. They say truth is not a straight line. It is like a line drawn around a ball; the beginning and the end could be the same point. Even though most people think that life is a celebration and we are here to make the most of it, Nora chose to end her life in a wilful act of taking it away herself.

Learned sages have mentioned that committing suicide disturbs the life-birth processes. The consciousness that is present in all of us, if forcefully taken away, is forced to go to another reality where the soul is stuck for a long time, as it is not able to take rebirth in another body. Some people might call that reality Hell. Some other learned people have also said that suicide occurs when a person has craved life so much that they cannot continue to live it any more. It is as if you have gambled away your life because your craving got to be too much. Indeed then, one would expect that the departure of soul from your body, when it was not supposed to leave based on your karmas, would make the soul linger in a stage of reality where it does not have a chance to redeem its ills. If people do choose to take away their lives, it is likely their karma.

If I have chosen to be a member of my profession as a physician it is my dharma to help save lives. Nora and I were both following our truth. It was as if her karma won because she chose to take her life; her free will persisted and she was successful. The debate on what could have been done differently, or whether what happened was right or wrong will continue. Hopefully my spirituality will help. Perhaps, you, as the reader, could reflect on this too and share your thoughts with me.

.And lastly, may I direct some of your reading time towards further thinking, reflecting, and contemplating on your very true nature. When I say YOUR true nature, I am also thinking of MY own nature. I cannot be different from you. We are all part of the same consciousness. That is the basic knowledge, which will help us get enlightened right now. Our nature is the all-powerful energy source, which is in everything; alive and dead, happiness and sadness, and all other opposites that we can see, feel, hear and, perceive. It is only during various sadhana practices like meditation and reading of knowledge that we recognize our true knowledge is this Infinite Self. So let us walk on this Earth with small steps that do not leave an imprint on the world. Let us not be agitated about earning money, our behaviour towards other people, or worrying about right from wrong. Our true nature is joy, fullness, contentment and stillness, which are all infinite. Anything and everything else are events that our sense organs are perceiving, time is shaping, and memory is making us remember. Let us just root ourselves to our true nature and the Infinite will give us the intuition and courage to do what is right. Let us drop all thoughts that we are different from each other. Let us think, reflect, contemplate, and pray on this thought.

CHAPTER 5. Anxiety

IT IS WELL KNOWN THAT ANXIETY IS ONE OF THE MOST COMMON mental health issues across the age spectrum. It is understandable as to why that might be. As adults we feel pressured to perform better at work and we try to outdo what our friends and neighbours have achieved in terms of accessories of life. As parents we feel under stress to get our children into the best schools; we worry about what grades they are going to get; about the extra-curricular activities that they need to complete so that they can excel; and about the college that they need to go to. We worry about the health of our parents, about financial savings being enough for retirement, and so on and so forth. As we get older we start worrying about our physical health, and then there's the worry about not having enough to sustain ourselves, and worrying about our kids and grandkids. It seems as if wherever we look, the whole world somehow seems to need to worry. As if worrying will cure the world of its problems.

When anxiety gets really bad, to where it starts to affect our function, people have no option but to seek some medical treatment. And we as physicians do not have the best treatments to offer to them. Till recently, I found anxiety disorders the most difficult to treat. Antidepressants do not seem to be that effective. People get addicted to benzodiazepines, though they work very well. As a geriatric psychiatrist I find them the best available treatment, but they have disastrous consequences. People taking them feel confused, they fall, break a hip, and land in nursing homes. Cognitive behaviour therapy works but you need to be motivated to follow through with the suggestions of the therapist. Psychodynamic therapy does not always work, as it seems to rely on concepts of having a missing parent or some sort of trauma, which made one feel the way that one feels now. Even if we were to find the source of the trauma, trying to work through it might not necessarily produce the expected benefits.

Now more than ever do we really need to understand the spiritual basis of this fear that we carry in our minds. The stress that anxiety carries with us is enormous, it is time that we "let-go."

So can Vedanta help? Indeed it can.

I will come back to my own story for a moment. When I was in medical school in India I started to have classical symptoms of anxiety and panic. I would have difficulty in going off to sleep in the night, my mind would be racing. I hated to be put on the spot where I had to perform a random song as part of my ragging. I had jitters in talking to my teachers, especially the ones from the anatomy department, as I just could not seem to remember the details of the arteries and veins. I could not talk to any of the good-looking girls in class. I became extremely shy. Of course, when I met my fiancée, things got so much better. These feelings seemed to whither away as she became my strength. Additionally, finding friends that I could really depend on and doing a lot of outdoor activities that I enjoyed did help tremendously. But for some reason I just could not completely relax.

My mother has a Sikh background. It was a tradition in her family that the eldest son always wore the turban and became a Sikh even though the rest of the family maintained Hindu customs and traditions. Some people might not be aware of this tradition. Other people might not be aware that Sikhism grew as an offshoot of Hinduism more as a necessity than a pure religion. The great saints of Sikhism were mostly warriors. Sikhs believe in achieving salvation through noble deeds and actions. This is very similar to what The Gita, the holy book of the Hindus might suggest too. Sikhism grew as an essential requirement. Under some of the emperors of the Moghul Empire, there was significant genocide of the Hindus. Sikhs developed martial arts to perfection and became the fiercest warriors that the world has ever known. Even now the Sikh regiment in the Indian Army is best known for its valour and courage.

Sikhism has the deepest and one of the simplest spiritual beliefs of any religion. I grew up listening to the gurubani (the words of the guru) in Punjabi, though I could not speak the language much. A lot of my friends in medical college were either Sikhs or spoke Punjabi. Having fun, respecting the Lord, offering service, was natural to all Sikhs and it felt natural to associate with them. The only time that I found complete peace and tranquillity during my medical school years was when I would go to the *gurudwara* (the gate to the guru or the Lord) in Connaught Place, New Delhi. I was inevitably there once every week, and daily just before the exams. I just felt the need to be there and could not explain what pulled me there. It felt as if each bhajan sung to the guru would reverberate inside me and huge feelings of compassion and peace rose through me. Doubts and worries just seemed to lift so easily, at least for the time that I was there in the temple. Having food from the common mess, called the *langar* was quite enriching, not only because of its simplicity but because it felt as if the guru had prepared all the food and everyone who ate it would feel lighter.

The more I think about this, I realize that there is something about prayer that helps us in letting go of our desires and attachments. Singing devotional songs or just being in the presence of people who are pouring out their hearts to the Divine can be uplifting. The value of prayer became established in my mind in my early years. I still go to each gurudwara in every city that I have the opportunity to visit.

I now know that the sole mission of my life is finding my true Self and service to humanity. Until only a little while ago, I was constantly riddled with thoughts generated by my ego. Even if I was gaining new knowledge I found myself comparing it to what I had previously learned. I was ignorant to the point where I thought that I knew everything, and so saw no point in learning anything new. I thought it was enough to know the fact that we all are born, we all are going to die, and nobody knows where we go after we die. So what is this Vedanta business? Who cares about what happens to us after we die? All we really need to do to is to live life meaningfully, get a job, respond to our families and their needs, earn a decent living, and the rest will all be fine. But, as I have shared with you before, the loss of my dad, the constant stress at work, of not being able to get a particular research grant, or not being able to get along with a particular colleague, the incessant demands of looking after the children's needs, including their classes, homework etc. was literally causing a din in my head. I was feeling incomplete and worried and anxious very easily. If I, as a psychiatrist, could not keep my thoughts, emotions, and feelings under control, I realized that quite a few people out there without scientific or spiritual knowledge might have similar problems.

Fast forward to Canada 2013. I had the opportunity to complete a course called the Art of Meditation through the Art of Living Foundation. Prior to this I was a big sceptic of meditation or any other spiritual technique. My wife suggested that there was no harm in trying the program out. She had just completed it and felt that she had made some sort of a connection with the course and its teachings.

My life changed dramatically after the course. Something moved in me. I had, for some strange reason, tears rolling down my eyes during the process. I felt I was letting go of my pent-up feelings of loss. By this time, my dad had been dead for more than four years and I thought I had grieved enough. Clearly that was not true. Waves of emotions welled up in me as if a dam had been breached. I had no control and sobbed uncontrollably for nearly an hour. It was so relieving.

In the past, whenever I had looked at the picture of my father in his full army uniform with his stripes and medals, I had feelings of upset, anger, and even hatred that he had left me. He had not even said goodbye to me. He had no right to be leaving his family at such a young age. After the meditation course, I felt a strange sense of calm whenever I looked at his picture. I could look at it with a peaceful sense of belongingness. It was as if I had finally let go of him.

My night's sleep became much more settled. My wife had always complained that I was a very light sleeper. Just a slight movement by her in bed would wake me up. After the course I could go off to sleep within minutes, if not seconds and would not wake up for at least six hours. Nothing seemed to wake me up in the middle of the night.

Prior to the course I would be a bit apprehensive about my ongoing research projects and grant applications. I'd ruminate about my complicated patients or the teaching activities that I had to plan, and all of these things made me feel anxious. But my pride and ego would prevent me discussing these feelings even with my wife. Yes, I would have a one-to-one conversation over a glass of wine with her, but words of support from her did not necessarily take away the tightness in my tummy or the feelings of ill ease that I had got so accustomed to. I needed regular therapeutic massages every few weeks. My masseur would say to me that the muscles in my back were always tense and it was good that I was coming to her frequently. Good business for her, surely!

After doing the course, I started to meditate once a day. In the first few weeks it was extremely challenging as my mind would wander so much. The teachers of the meditation program had warned the course participants that we should not expect that our minds would be completely at ease. Rather, we were encouraged to let the thoughts come in, observe them, and then let them go. Our teachers encouraged us to focus on our breath whenever our thoughts became too much. We were just to notice the breath coming in through the nose, inflate the lungs, moving our diaphragm, and feel the energy associated with each inhalation. Then we could focus on our exhalation and feel the cool, relaxing air passing through our nostrils. I regularly practiced meditation, twice a day, and over the next few months I noticed I was able to go into deeper states of relaxation during each meditation session.

After a few months I completed an additional Art of Silence course. The course was designed as a four-day retreat in which we would do gentle yoga every morning, listen to a lot of spiritual knowledge and learn newer meditation techniques. We were more than adequately provided for throughout the course. We had fresh meals prepared on site and remained in silence through the day and night. We were asked to simply immerse ourselves in the technique without any judgment or preconceived ideas. At an average we would go through meditation eight times a day with each session lasting an hour; each a bit different from the other.

Somehow the whole body was being gently massaged. And it cried. I was in so much pain. All my muscles and joints ached. If it were not for the yoga I would have run away from the course. The yoga-asanas helped the body feel completely loose and at ease and we could easily immerse ourselves into each meditation session.

After each meditation I felt the silence was deafening. I could feel the breeze on my face literally touching every nerve ending. I could feel the body getting calmer every day. Something magical was happening. By the end of the course I felt extremely light, as if floating in air. I felt as if I had been detoxified from all the worries, despair, obsessions, and bad habits.

I subsequently went on a holiday to Acapulco, Mexico with my family. We own a time-share in a resort chain in Mexico, which allows us to choose any resort in the main tourist spots across either the Atlantic or Pacific coasts. Blessed are we that so far our family has been able to enjoy the worldly pleasures while I still have been able to continue to remain steadfastly on the spiritual journey.

I now wish to share my experiences on that holiday. I took it onto myself to read a book called the *Autobiography of a Yogi* by Swami Paramhansa Yogananda. I have always been an early riser, so it was not hard for me to get up at around 3:45 a.m. I read a few chapters every day before the family awoke from their slumber. The experiences of Swami Ji somehow struck a deep chord inside me. His basic upbringing, his silly pranks in childhood, his interests at a young age in finding liberation, his encounters with many enlightened beings all across India were all captivating and alluring. Something seemed to shift in my consciousness after reading those wonderful chapters. I was, as they call it, hooked! I started to believe that I too could be a yogi who could unravel the depths and secrets of this life.

His Grace flowed during those days. I had never had such experiences. On the first day I was out golfing with my daughter. I had the best round ever. My concentration was impeccable. After every shot, all the golf balls went exactly where I had intended them to go. There was something magical happening; I knew I was not the best golfer. Rather, whenever I had played with my dad or colleagues I had always allowed my mind to take over my shots. I knew that I was the worst putter and had the most dismal drives off the green, though I could be consistent in the rest of the game. (If anybody has played golf, they know that putting and the first shot are usually the most crucial. So yes, previous to that day I had been a miserable golfer!)

However, somehow that day I was very calm, and life seemed much more relaxed. The next day, when we went to play our next round of golf, something even more magical happened. I felt very strange and blissful. Huge waves of happiness started to envelope me. This is very difficult for me to write as language is one of our biggest barriers in communication, but here is an attempt.

I felt that I was the whole world and I was full of energy. I felt as if the whole world was being consummated by me. Not just all human beings but each and every aspect of the creation. Be it a coconut tree, the ocean, or even the air. Each and every cell of my body was consummating everything. I was in perfect unity with the rest of the world. Wherever I put my foot on the ground it felt supremely light, as if I was walking on air. I was caressing Mother Earth and she was caressing me.

I was dumbstruck. I knew I had not consumed any hallucinogen! I had stopped drinking alcohol more than two years ago, so no drink could have been spiked. We were consuming food bought from the supermarket and cooked in our own kitchen, so the food could not have been spiked either. I felt physically at 100%, if not more. I knew that I was not getting manic; I had full insight into what was going on. This could be nothing but the Divine's grace flowing through Swami Ji's book and his wonderful words.

Such experiences came and went for nearly four days.

I also found it very strange that we had chosen Acapulco as our holiday destination. There were hardly any tourists there because of some recent high-profile murders. However, I knew I could have easily passed as a native Mexican with my Asian looks and a moustache. I knew I would be safe. Such a faith likely had come from my dad who had previously taken us deep in the jungles in rebel tribal areas all across India. I had also seen much strife in Delhi during the assassination of our prime minister, Srimati (Mrs.) Indira Gandhi in 1984, and a few gun shots or a few houses being burnt down here and there was definitely more gruesome than hearing that there had been a few homicides between gang members in Acapulco. It is indeed bizarre that I had these blissful experiences in that city in that part of the world. Perhaps the forefathers of previous civilizations had a role to play in those experiences as well. I don't know.

What I do know now is that this stage of bliss is likely what enlightened people go through all the time, not just for four days. These souls are rooted in this wonderful consciousness, the Self, which pervades everyone and everything. There are many accounts of enlightened people and their experiences if we look hard enough. Yes, there may be some recluses in some parts of the world, but there are also many enlightened souls all over the modern world doing their great deeds to help everyone. With the wonderful technology available to us all now, we can search for their deeds on our laptops. It is likely that you are reading this book on a tablet or a computer, which has access to the whole wide world. Isn't that itself a source of awe, wonder, and a manifestation of the Divine – that he gave the intelligence to a few souls so that we can share this knowledge and do great deeds for the rest of humanity? I am constantly dumbstruck with so many people in the corporate and charitable world giving so much back to the community. Thanks to the Internet we are able to scour the knowledge available out there, seek great souls, talk to them via Facebook and Twitter, and feel so wonderfully calm in ourselves that maybe, we can make a difference to this world too.

We soon returned from our holiday and I have kept my experiences a secret till now. The only reason I am sharing it with everyone at this point is because I have an inner calling of some kind. I am aware, like you, that I have suffered and there is too much suffering in this world. Mental illness is just the ego keeping a big lid on one's true potential, the supreme consciousness or one's true nature. It was only by God's grace that I had such an awakening. I had done nothing special, so far as I know, to be in His Grace and to have such experiences. But just having these experiences suggests to me that this knowledge needs to be shared.

From the depth of the misery of various mental illnesses, many people have come out calm, truthful, virtuous, effulgent, and shining. I have heard many life stories recently of other people finding peace in the depth of their misery, after being in contact with a holy soul, or even just finding it within themselves. I knew it was very important to communicate this intelligence that has been offered to me by the Divine Self. I just had to share my story, share the knowledge gained so far, share my experiences so far...and hence this book.

Over the last couple of years my life has changed so much. I know that this will continue if I remain virtuous and hard working and continue to follow my spiritual practices. I now have no tension about working with the "difficult" patient. Such a person needs more compassion from me rather than less. I am very lucky to be able to make a connection with most people in even the most complex situations. I had read a great deal about ego-boundaries, self-regulation, negative automatic thoughts, schemas, and similar concepts during my training and now started to realise that these are alien concepts from the point of view of the patient. In the mental health field, we use such concepts to talk amongst ourselves, but this does not necessarily lead to an improvement in our interaction with our patients nor does it seem to help them recover from their illnesses. We use these ideas more as a way of distancing ourselves from them, rather than being with them. Compassion, warmth in our interaction, and truthfulness are all a patient needs. Trust and faith then develop automatically.

Over the last few months it feels to me as if each patient's worry is simple to understand and appreciate. Just being there with my patients, listening to them attentively, offering them simple words of wisdom, doing some simple breathing exercises, and meditating with them seems much more effective than prescribing medications or trying complex psychotherapies.

Life has started to feel much easier at work and it is now a joy to interact with all of my colleagues. Slowly, I have learned to feel much more at ease with people whom I once did not get along with very well. Now, if somebody touches a raw nerve in me, I examine that feeling, laugh at it and quickly realize the need to move on. I recognize that everybody has a right to his or her own thoughts. It is the nature of human beings to think. So how can one person's thoughts be pure versus another person's being impure? As long as the intention is correct then everything is good. We find differences between the next person and ourselves only because of our egos, our memories, or our past impressions. It is important to just let go of the ego when it is causing a problem. Egos have a role in establishing new ideas and motivating us to work; that is it. Otherwise, the only reason egos exist is to provide material for various soap operas on the idiot box. Through my active practice of spiritual principles, I started to recognize much more easily when my ego was causing a problem and I understood the need to continuously dampen it through more Seva and Satsanga.

I felt the need to work with no expectations from my actions. Simply accepting every activity as a source of joy made it joyful. All failures appeared as exercises in learning rather than sources of despair or anxiety about future prospects. Slowly, intuition was taking a foothold in me. I could start to anticipate what the other person was thinking, even before they spoke it. I have now started to feel the need to speak less and do more. Knowing your limit and saying NO becomes so much easier. I feel much calmer yet more assertive when I know that something is not right.

The odd feelings in my tummy are now gone. I feel younger every day in my mind though I am even more appreciative of how this body is aging right in front of my eyes.

I hope that you find a teacher who can help you meditate and follow through with practices. Let no one talk your peace away. Use prayer, knowledge, faith, and selfless service, as the motto that defines you, and you shall be at peace.

a) Meditation and The Principles of Truth

Now I wish to dispel some common misconceptions around meditation and describe a little bit about the principles of truth.

Meditation is about concentrating on my thoughts.

No, meditation involves keeping a light eye over our thoughts and emotions when we have our eyes shut. We don't need to concentrate on a particular thought but should keep a watchful vigil over our thoughts as they arise and go away. We will, of course, have good and bad thoughts, ruminative, anxious, and worrisome thoughts. The nature of the mind is to have thoughts, but we don't need to concentrate on them. The more you focus on a thought, the more it persists. It is a similar concept to when we are trying to sleep. If we want to make ourselves go off to sleep, we often are unable to do so because we become conscious that we are awake and our mind starts to feel too alert and wary.

I need to have a fixed time to meditate daily. If I have missed it, then I should not try to meditate that day, as it is likely not going to be effective.

Indeed, self-discipline helps one find the centeredness in our lives more easily. However, meditation is like an expression of our eternal love towards our Self. Do we need to love our loved ones at a certain time of the day? No. It just happens automatically at any time of the day or night. Similarly, you can meditate at any time of the day or night. Having a reasonably empty stomach, a quiet part of the house, and letting people know that you are going to need some silence for the next few minutes really helps them and yourself. Self discipline yourself in providing adequate sleep to your body. Find a comfortable seat and sit straight in your meditative posture. It is that simple.

Some people claim that they are meditating when they are lying in bed getting ready to sleep. I suspect that their quality of meditation will improve if they sit up and rest their backs comfortably on the bed. Having a relaxed and comfortable position to meditate is important; however, it is also important that we are awake enough to be able to go into a different level of consciousness through meditation.

It is necessary for me to meditate on a mantra or a hymn or music or a song.

There is some truth in this statement. Let me share with you an account of a patient whom I recently saw. For treatment of symptoms of depression, her family doctor referred her to me. Typically, on our team, we ask that a psychiatry nurse or a social worker do the initial assessment. This really helps the patient know more about our team, establishes rapport, and helps the psychiatrist know about the symptoms more quickly. Thus we can plan our treatment even before the patient walks into the room. I was surprised to hear that this patient would not agree to meet our nurse and only wanted to meet me. That does not happen frequently and it made me curious.

On the day of her appointment, the patient came in and after a few minutes spent on introductions she acknowledged that she was no longer depressed. I was surprised and curious as to why this person wished to see a specialist and wondered how her symptoms had gone away. She shared that over the last few months since the referral she had started to use some mantra- based meditation techniques, which are freely available through YouTube. I was truly amazed to hear this and asked her to elaborate, but she did not feel comfortable enough to share which particular technique she had found. At this point, she only needed me for helping her with her benzodiazepine dependence issues. I hope I was able to provide for her needs. Later in the evening, my curiosity remained and I searched YouTube for various meditation techniques. It was mind-boggling to discover what people have uploaded there. There was such a wealth of information, and all for free. Perhaps the woman I had just met had found her guru through a particular video and that had cured her of her depression. I was truly happy for her.

Coming back to the question of whether we need to meditate on a mantra or not, I must confess that I have not found the answer to this one yet. What I do recognize is that on some days my meditation is very deep and profound, especially when I have tried to help as many people as I can selflessly. I can go into a deep state of relaxation very quickly. On other days, the mind just does not settle, and on those days mantras really help in focusing the mind. In the Art of Meditation course that I took a few months ago, during the various processes that we underwent during the course, the teachers privately offered each participant a particular mantra, which was just a small sound value; just one vowel and one consonant. We were instructed to use this mantra whenever our minds wandered during meditation and were instructed not to tell anyone what it was as it was special to us alone. It was a sacred binding to the Divine. We were invited to keep our faith. And indeed I have tried to keep the faith in using my mantra during my meditation and it really helps.

On days that I have felt really grateful I have tried to use other mantras or chants and they do help in meditating. Everybody will likely find a particular chant, mantra, or hymn that really reverberates with his or her own energy and mood state. Try out a few for yourself and then use them every time for your continued growth.

Meditation is our very nature and the surest way of reaching the Divine Self. With this knowledge, practice meditation daily and you will notice wonders happening every day. And when you do, accept them and offer them back to the Divine. And on the days that you do not have that great an experience, do not blame yourself. Have no expectations for and during the meditation. This is the basic rule.

I need to sit for at least twenty minutes in meditation, twice a day, every day.

No, this is not a requirement but a suggested time. As you become more experienced you will realize that you can even meditate with your eyes open. The more experienced meditators have fewer thoughts in their minds, there are no worrying thoughts, there is less need to make "plans" for the day or for the future, things happen by themselves, and thoughts come only for noble deeds. People become much more productive, they don't feel the need to gossip, and a feeling of contentment arises in every part of the day.

An experienced teacher has said that there are only three rules of meditation. They are: I do nothing. I want nothing. I am nothing. Each of these three components is profound. Reflect on each before you read any further. Do not expect yourself to be doing anything during meditation, do not wish something for yourself or your family as a blessing during meditation, and do not think of yourself during meditation.

May, I suggest a couple of wonderful links about the power of mantras

1. https://www.youtube.com/watch?v=kf_2sh-kMyU (Link provides Om Namah Shivaya chanting.)
2. https://youtu.be/qOfNUcShgbw (Link provides information on the power of noise and mantras on crystal formation.)

b) Consciousness and Meditation

We all, at any stage of our lives, are going through three states of consciousness: We are awake, dreaming, or in deep sleep. In the wakeful state, our minds are the most active with a constant barrage of thoughts and constant seeking of new impulses to satisfy our sense organs. Have you also noticed that the words "sense" and "sensual" are quite similar, as if all our sense organs are always seeking something sensual, something attractive and yet illusory?

Have we not all had a feeling of complete let-down after having had an orgasm? Such a big high at the time of climax and then a deep fall into an abyss where everything is gloomy. That is the power of the mind. The mind is literally a roller coaster of highs and lows with happy and sad thoughts, distasteful and tasty morsels of food, pleasant and unpleasant smells, and every other contrast that you can imagine. It just can't seem to relax or be calm.

Our dream state is even more perplexing. We are constantly making sand castles out of thin air. Each and every dream is so different. The concept of time becomes illusory in our dreams. Our experiences of the past and fantasies of the future get intertwined into a long or a short story. Often the stories do not make sense. Our minds are really running riot in this state of consciousness. Everything that we see in a dream or a fantasy can seem very real and we get sucked into accepting that indeed is the truth. (Of course whether we are actually "seeing" is questionable, because our eyes are shut, but we do know that the parts of the brain that perceive light; the occipital cortex and others, are indeed active in a dream.) How can a dream not be anything but somebody's playful idea? Maybe it is the Creator having fun and that is why He instilled in us these dreams.

The only time that we are really are at rest is during the stage of deep sleep. In this state the mind is calm, thoughts do not arise, and we can't feel or perceive any sensations. The concept of time seems to truly go away. Perhaps all we preserve is a sense of our Self during this stage of consciousness. So far, no one has understood well what really happens in our deep sleep. Even though the physiological functions are being maintained during deep sleep, our minds really do not know where we are, whether we are hot or cold, or whether we are alive or dead. Could this mean that this state of our consciousness is where we are closest to the Divine? It is said that the emptiness and hollowness that we find in deep sleep is what is actual reality; the unchangeable, the truth.

Meditation allows us to transcend these three states of consciousness. When we begin our meditation, we initially shut our eyes and sit in a relaxed posture; our minds are, however, still very active. Our thoughts and feelings are still arising in us. Our intellect is also reasonably sharp as we are able to understand that we are not asleep, and we can differentiate between the good and the bad thoughts. In the next state of meditation, we might find ourselves fantasizing about some events. This is similar to what we experience in a dream state. The intellect is active in this state but the mind has quieted. Then our minds become even quieter as we go into a deeper state of relaxation. This state is akin to deep sleep but perhaps not. The quality is somewhat different. Some sages have therefore called it *turiya* or the fourth state of consciousness (besides the waking, dream, and deep sleep states). This is where we find complete stillness and emptiness. Experienced meditators are able to get into this state very quickly.

I find it very interesting that the harder you try to go into a deeper state of relaxation during meditation, the harder it is to actually reach a deep state. The mind starts to work like a barrier. The only way to achieve *turiya* is to completely let go of any expectations of the meditative practice. There is one basic rule for anyone on the spiritual journey: Do not expect anything, demand anything, or plan for anything. Just do things spontaneously and let your consciousness blossom. During the twenty-four hours of the day work hard, sleep adequately, read knowledge from the great masters, remain virtuous, stay in good company, help as many people as you can, and then let the magic begin.

During *turiya*, some people find themselves experiencing a Divine light or energy encompassing their whole bodies as if every cell of their bodies are fired up. They are full of vigour with a wonderfully warm feeling. For other people, or at other times during *turiya,* there might be the sensation of complete silence with no thoughts or feelings and a sense of departure from the body. Both states, I understand, are possible.

Sri Sri Ravi Shankar mentions that our natural state is stillness and emptiness. During his Art of Silence Advanced Course he specifically teaches how to achieve complete stillness using his "Hollow and Empty" meditations.

Perhaps that is what the Divine wants us to try during the alert states of consciousness – no expectations of anything, anyone, or any time. Then we will find bliss even in the alert and dreaming states. So let us practice equanimity, selflessness, awareness, centeredness, truthfulness, sincerity, and compassion at every moment and we will have no choice but to get enlightened.

Various masters through the ages have shown that meditation increases awareness of our environment and surroundings. Many accounts exist of people who have gone into deep states of meditation to the point where surgical operations could be conducted without the need of anaesthesia. If you were to meet regular meditators they would share with you that minor illnesses do not seem to affect them any more. Their tolerance to pain has also increased. Sri Sri Ravi Shankar teaches that when we raise our consciousness and awareness during meditation, we become more aware of the sensations that are happening in the body and we see that the sensations change. An intense sensation that is pain and an intense sensation that is pleasure, both become pleasurable.

I would like to offer an example of using the mind to your own advantage during meditation. After being an experienced meditator for the last couple of years, I still find myself noticing an itch or some pain in my body. I would like to share a wonderful trick that I have learned to help me get into a deeper state of meditation. Whenever I feel that a particular part of the body is either itching or in pain, I trick the mind to think that my whole body is itching or is in pain. Within a few seconds I can feel those sensations throughout the body. However, within the next few seconds, all these irritant sensations just dissipate. It is as if the storm literally takes away the minor irritant. Try it out!

I have also learnt another technique, which you could consider incorporating into your meditation routine. We have previously read about the breath being the central part of the connection between the body, mind, and intellect. All emotions are connected through the breath. That is a given. During various meditation techniques like mindfulness or kriya we are encouraged to simply notice our breath and change it to allow us into a deeper state of consciousness. So, just by plain logic, if there is a Divine energy, which is within all of us and knows what is the best for us and our bodies, minds, and intellect equipment, why don't we let that Divine self take control of our breath as well? If we can let go of our bad thoughts and emotions through meditation, perhaps in meditation we should also just let go of our breath. This might sound radical and on the verge of insanity but I thought, what the heck! It came as a revelation to me and I did try it out a few days ago. The sensations arising during such meditation sessions have truly been amazing. It is as if the Divine knows exactly and what rate of breathing is important to help me move into a deeper state of relaxation or energy based on the need for the day. If I have not slept well, my breath takes me to a deeper state of relaxation that is just like deep sleep. If I am full of tamas (lethargy) on a particular morning, my breath helps me provide so much energy that literally my whole head is pounding and my whole body is shaking with energy. If I am in a sattvik (relaxed) mode, then the breath helps me go into a deep state where I can literally feel the breath cooling the back of my throat, my nose tingling with energy, and my chest heaving while my mind completely at ease. Heavenly!

During the Art of Silence course, participants are encouraged to think about an expansion of the mind during meditation. This is a very interesting concept that needs to be further explored. Our current concept of the mind is that it is present within the brain. However, as of now, modern science cannot prove that the mind actually resides in the brain.

In fact, let me suggest to you some very simple experiments to confirm that the mind could be somewhere outside the brain. First, have you not noticed that when you are just observing someone and thinking about them, watching them from the rear, they may sense that you are observing them and actually turn back and look towards you? This especially occurs when you have positive intentions toward them, not angry or dirty intentions. Next time that you are in a shopping mall or on a bus stop, do try this experiment. Just start having positive thoughts about somebody. Lo and behold, you will notice within a few seconds he or she will look back towards you. Unreal!

This experiment's success logically proves that our minds can "sense" that another person is thinking about us. If our minds are just the brain, then all that this mind can perceive is the information from our eyesight coming from our optical nerves to our occipital cortexes. However, in this experiment we never let the other person know that we are thinking about them or looking at them. The mind is nothing but consciousness, and it has to reside in, as well as, outside the brain.

Now let us try another one, but this time it will be a meditative experiment. For the best result I would suggest that you perform this experiment as soon as you have read this paragraph. Go into a part of your home that you know is quiet. Then sit in a contemplative, meditative resting position with your eyes closed.

Imagine that you are in a special place; where no sound can travel as there are no air particles to carry the waves; where no light can travel as there are no photonsenergy-carrying ability; where gravity cannot exert its effect as there are no gravitons or other sub-atomic particles that are responsible for gravity; where there is no concept of time as time has come to a stand-still; where thoughts cannot exist as there is no mind to carry the thoughts; where there is no colour, smell, depth, shape, size or texture; where there is nothingness. It is untouched, unblemished, and infinite.

It might be that within a few seconds of your contemplation you actually do find yourself in a completely blank space, which is just like the description above. That stage is *samadhi* or where we are in touch with our consciousness. It is this place where our minds stop and everything else begins, yet there is nothing there. So, by logic, again, our minds cannot be in our brains. When we are in a supreme meditative nothingness everything as we know it disappears in the outer world.

Last fact/experiment: When we see ourselves in our dreams we always associate ourselves with a person who is usually younger in physical structure than the person whom we meet in the mirror the next morning. How is it possible that the mind is fooled in not acknowledging the ravages of time on the body?

The success of these simple experiments suggests to us that the mind is indeed complex and could be outside the brain. We do know that there are certain brain areas that are activated whilst we are receiving sensations from our sense organs, or when we're thinking, feeling, planning, or moving. But the mind is so much more than just these activities alone. It allows us, for instance, to have a sense of something that is going to happen to us or others (intuition). It also gives us the understanding and faith that whichever activity we embark upon is safe as well other wonderful concepts of humanity, which reside in us such as justice, ethics, and morality. Don't we have a "gut" feeling with all these "wooly" concepts? It is as if our brain depends on these concepts outside our cranium – as if it is somewhere in the gut or even outside our bodies.

When our consciousness gets elevated through meditation, the mind stops being stuck on anxious thoughts and it rather starts to listen to the nature around us. Our intuition rises. We can come to know of things that people are thinking as if we are reading their minds. Don't tell anyone, but this is true of all meditators. Keep this the best secret between you and me!!

In meditation the mind expands as well as relaxes. I quote Sri Sri Ravi Shankar:

> *Whenever you are happy, you feel that something in you is expanding.*
>
> *Whenever you are relaxed, you are expanding automatically.*
>
> *It is worth knowing this expansion – because then nothing can disturb you, or take your smile away.*
>
> *Otherwise, some small things can throw you off balance. Expression of sadness is the contraction of the mind. It is not worth letting your mind or your life undergo such suffering, such misery.*

With meditation arises intuitive awareness. This intuitive quotient always comes to your help. If you lack intuition, you can't be really successful! Intuition is not just dry thinking.

In his commentary on Patanjali Yogasutras, Sri Sri Ravi Shankar says: "[With spiritual growth], there is a keenness of observation. You become totally relaxed, yet at the same time you possess sharpness of awareness, strength of intelligence. Your senses become so clear. You can see better, think better, and hear better. Like a pure crystal, your senses come to reflect all objects as one Divinity."

c) The Neurological Science Behind Meditation

There is now an immense interest in investigating the neurobiological basis of the advantages of meditation. All these new and exciting findings will likely need a whole book by itself to do justice to the extent of the growing information. However, that is not the intention of this book. My aim is to provide the reader a snapshot, a bird's eye view, of the basics of spirituality and science behind Vedanta.

The knowledge available to us is vast; when we incorporate it into the working storehouse of our intellect, it becomes wisdom. Wisdom helps us grow spiritually and offers benefits of acceptance, calmness, and the courage to face all adversity. So here are some bite-sized bullet points for the scientific knowledge around meditation. Hopefully this will help increase the wisdom about meditation for all of humanity.

- There are various types of meditative practices. All of them are quite similar as far as the extent of their clinical benefits. However, there are subtle differences in the processes of delivery, the ease of delivery, and the meditator's ability to follow through with the teacher's instruction.
- All meditative practices generally lead to calming of the body as measured by blood pressure, heart rate, heart rate variability, stress markers (like cortisol), improvement in immune status, and anti-ageing effects. Generally speaking, there are acute benefits noticed just after completing a meditative session, but recent studies also suggest sustained benefits over time.
- Magnetic Resonance Imaging (MRI) has seen a lot of innovation over the past few years, which allows us to measure the minute details of individual nerve tracts, their supporting structures, and the rate of blood flow in various parts of the brain as well as the connectivity of nerves between various brain areas. The most interesting finding from neuroimaging studies so far, in my humble opinion, is our enhanced ability to use more parts of our brain when we meditate regularly. Most people are able to use only twenty to thirty percent of their brain at any time. We have something called the default mode network, which is activated when we are reflecting on matters that involve ourselves or our emotions. We have another extrinsic network, which gets activated when we are doing something physically active like watching sports or having a cup of coffee. In most people we are able to use either of these networks (of nerve connections), but never at the same time, hence

the low usage of our total brain capacity. In experienced meditators, though, it has now been shown that both networks become active while the subjects are meditating. Other studies show that in meditators the white matter (the covering around the nerve cells) integrity also improves markedly and continues to do so over time. The effects have been likened to laying new white matter as happens in all of us from childhood to adolescence. So literally, the brain becomes younger with regular meditation.

d) The Truth

Various religions and scriptures expound upon the Truth. By the truth I do not refer to the quality of a human being to speak the truth, which is a virtuosity we all should learn and maintain.

I am referring to the ultimate question: Who Am I?

If we look at the building blocks of this whole creation as described by the ancient seers in the Upanishads and the Brahmasutras, it seems to be made of only five elements. Everywhere that these eyes see, the ears hear, our feet touch or we taste seems to be Earth, Fire, Water, Air and Ether. The sages mention that these elements form the creation and they are the creation. This includes our body, mind and intellect. Everything.

Let us explore this concept a bit more. If my mind is agitated, angry, or annoyed then likely the fire element in my body is arising. Hence my body feels warm or even hot, my heart is pounding and I cannot think straight. So both my body and mind are activated with this fire element. If we now look at this microscopically there are likely specific changes happening in various neurochemicals in the brain, the heart, and the cardiovascular system, to generate some heat by raising the heart rate and the blood pressure. But we don't just keep getting hot and angry. A stage comes when these physiological conditions get stabilized. This is likely because the water element cools down the body.

We can, by our intellect, understand that certain permutations of the various elements lead to the formation and dissolution of most emotions.

So am I these five elements? Is that what I am?

Yes, you are and no, you are not. These elements are the building blocks of creation. As a person you can see, feel, hear, touch, and taste; but, who IS the entity behind these senses? You are likely just an observer of the sensations they produce. We notice the object that we are observing. But who is the experiencer?

Let us reflect further on this. This creation likely exists at multiple levels. Perhaps a part of it is in an area where our sense organs cannot yet take us. But we can still experience it somewhat. The extreme calmness that we experience when we are completely still and have no thoughts, feelings or perceptions is likely the Source or the Consciousness. This is the emptiness which was well described by Gautama Buddha and other enlightened souls. This is the source from where all creation arose, and it includes the five elements. We have also previously referred it to as a source of Energy or the Divine. Or OM, the primordial sound.

New research has shown some very interesting findings. If we try to listen to the sound coming from our sun, we will not hear anything, as there are no particles to transmit the sound waves. Instruments taken into space at a distance far away from our earth have picked up electromagnetic waves in the vacuum of space. These instruments have been able to modulate the frequency of these sound waves so that the human ear can hear them. Interestingly, some of the sound emanating from the sun, and likely from other stars in the universe is similar to the Om sound suggested by the Vedanta seers. So we can deduce that this sound or mantra, Om, is the primordial sound and all the languages spoken by human beings as well as noises created by animals are permutations and combinations of this mantra. For that reason it is also called the maha mantra, or the great mantra.

Om is present everywhere and hence it embodies emptiness in the macroscopic and the microscopic world. This emptiness, by its nature, is infinite.

So how can we define the infinite by mere finite words or experience it with the limited five senses, which have been powered through the five elements provided to us? The seers say that this source of energy is what we are all made of and everything else dissolves into.

More and more research points out that there is complete emptiness everywhere. If we look at the physical body that we each have, and examine it microscopically there is nothing but emptiness in the cells, the atoms, and the sub-atomic particles. Some very interesting experiments in quantum mechanics are the most puzzling and are pointing out that this emptiness controls everything that we can see and perceive. Our efforts to find out more about sub-atomic particles makes them appear just because we are looking for them. This is a very strange phenomenon that quantum mechanic scientists are unable to explain fully. In the words of Werner Heisenberg, one of the leaders in this science, "The atoms or elementary particles are not real, they form a world of potentialities rather than one of things or facts."

If we look outside the body, into the bigger universes and galaxies, research is pointing out that there is definitely more empty space than cosmic bodies. And this empty space itself regulates and keeps the cosmic bodies together. What we perceive as gravity, that which brings the proverbial apple down from the tree, is such a small energy compared to the dark matter that keeps all the cosmic bodies together. This dark matter is complete emptiness.

Additionally, very briefly, I would like to point the reader toward wonderful research confirming that there are likely some other universes outside the ones that we can see and perceive. Taking into account the treatises of those who have had near-death experiences, it is impossible to even logically fathom that we do not go "somewhere" after we all die. All the space agencies constantly looking for other life forms within this universe could potentially be flawed. We would likely need another mode of "transport" besides radio, gamma, and infrared waves, as they are unable to penetrate the effect of time and distance. Just by gross logic it is completely impossible not to have other parallel universes. Science fiction continues to flourish with concepts of time travel and parallel universes because we simply do not have an answer yet. But we remain in the hope that somehow, with our current technologies, we will be able to detect life-forms on other planets and in other universes. Such noble aspirations! However, the answer, as alluded to above, is very simple.

The whole of creation is consciousness, which is created in the Infinite and dissolves in the Infinite.

Let us talk a little bit about the fears that trouble us all. Some common themes for fears that I have myself heard of and used to have, are our worries about the future, the well being of our families, and having enough nourishment, wealth, and health to sustain us the rest of our lives. But if you listen a bit more closely to people expressing these fears, then you hear them talking about feeling scared of dying. Death defies understanding by these logical and analytical minds of ours. So many books and theses have been written to try to unravel death, but they come very short of providing clear-cut answers. The knowledge of death is the basis of spirituality. In the next few paragraphs I hope to share some knowledge that I have recently gained from reading the *Katha Upanishad.*

Let me tell you the story of Nachiketa. This story is thousands of years old. Nachiketa was an innocent, eleven-year-old boy born into the family of an ascetic, wealthy, and altruistic family. His father knew the advantage of giving away worldly possessions as he had learnt how important it is not to keep hoarding things, as we are not going to take them with us after our journey through this world is over.

Nachiketa, like any child, loved his father very much and really looked up to him. In his innocence, one day he noticed that his father was giving away mostly old clothes rather than new clothes. He pointed out to his father that if he were to receive those clothes he would likely not wear them. His father realized his mistake. On another day, his father was giving away a lot of other possessions and it was turning out to be a very busy day. Nachiketa wanted to talk to his father, but his father was very engrossed and Nachiketa just could not get a word in. The boy had a burning desire to help his dad dispose of all his things and he had a simple question in his mind. "If my dad is giving away all that he possesses, then he should give me away too." So he asked his dad, "Dad, when are you going to give me away?"

He kept asking and his father did not reply. Nachiketa persisted and finally his father relented and said, "Go away, I give you away to death."

At that very instant Nachiketa's soul departed his body and it arose to the supreme Divine abode. Some of us call this place Heaven. It is said that Nachiketa sat on the doorsteps of Heaven, which are controlled by Yama, the lord of death. Yama wished to check Nachiketa's level of patience, an absolutely important virtue for anyone who is a seeker. After four days, Yama came to the gates to fetch Nachiketa and asked him what he was doing there. In his innocence the boy replied that dad wished him to be dead so he was here as per his father's command. He was calm and composed when he said this. Yama was moved extremely by his innocence. The lord knew that Nachiketa was ordained to live a much longer life, but his soul was so pure that it had no option but to depart from the boy's body after hearing the order to die from his father. Yama offered any boon that Nachiketa wished to have, but also ordered him to go back to his father, as his time to die had not arrived yet.

The conversation between the death lord and Nachiketa is beautifully described in the *Katha Upanishad*. Yama mentions to Nachiketa how this whole world is illusory, and is hence called *maya* in Sanskrit, and he tells him that we all have a certain age to live and then be reborn. Our impressions of this world and the virtues that we accumulate do influence how and where we will be reborn. As our souls are infinite, but our bodies have a limited life, the soul has to depart within a few seconds of death. Yama mentions that at the time of death, the sense organs withdraw first. We lose the ability to receive touch sensations as well as to move our bodies, and then we lose taste, then smell, then hearing, and finally our full eyesight. Then our breathing stops and lastly, the soul departs.

Nachiketa was also very interested to find out about liberation or *mukti* of the soul. He asks Yama how a person can be relieved of these repeated cycles of birth and death so that the Self rests in peace and in perfect tranquillity. After a lot of hesitation, Yama relents and explains that the only way of achieving liberation is by yoga i.e. spiritual practices, (which we have discussed before), and meditation.

Nachiketa is sent back to his father with his first wish fulfilled – that his dad accept him back willingly without any reprimands or anger. Yama was so happy with Nachiketa that he additionally offered him a number of other boons including *mukti* or liberation/enlightenment even whilst alive.

It is said that a person who gets enlightened recognizes the futility of life; of worldly possessions and the need to earn wealth, and the need to maintain the body and its desires. He who is enlightened is rooted in his own Self, accepting all that is offered to him as an experience, and he drinks the poison of life as nectar waiting to leave his body when his time comes. He fears not death or misery, nor does he revel in happiness. He accepts whatever comes to him as *Prasad* or Divine fruit. He finds the Divinity in everything. He hence has become enlightened or gained *mukti*.

Let us all aim to get enlightened within this lifetime. That is my sincerest wish for all the readers of this book. If the contents of this book have motivated you to get on the path, enhanced your knowledge, or given you motivation to apply this knowledge to your day, then its intention is fulfilled.

Let us now examine the science behind death: research conducted on people who have had near-death experiences or have had acute brain injuries does suggest that, at least at the level of the brain, consciousness does seem to retract in similar stages as described by Yama to Nachiketa. An example of such research is that conducted by Professor Adrian Owen, a colleague here in London, Ontario who is investigating various disorders of consciousness. Such disorders can be broadly sub-divided into those who are either in a "minimally conscious state" or "vegetative state." Both categories of patients are unable to respond to verbal commands because their motor ability to respond them has been lost. Yama had mentioned that the first stage of withdrawal of consciousness at the time of death is the loss of our ability to perceive external sensations and our motor ability. It is only later that we start to lose other sensations

118

such as hearing and vision. Now imagine the situation of a person who has had a head injury whose withdrawal of consciousness is stuck at the first level. Such people are no longer able to respond to touch, to move their bodies spontaneously, or to react to verbal commands. Even so, they are constantly aware of what is happening around them. Some of these patients are able to move their eyes but cannot speak. However, such patients do listen, though they have hitherto been unable to communicate. Using Functional Magnetic Resonance Imaging (fMRI) techniques as well as Electroencephalography (EEG) Professor Owen has been able to literally communicate with such patients. In his research he asks such patients to imagine particular activities, and with the fMRI the Professor can observe that this generates the predictable brain activation associated with a deliberate, conscious response. Specifically, in his fMRI studies he has asked patients to imagine playing tennis or navigating around their house. In EEG studies, he asks patients to imagine clenching their fists or wiggling their toes. These imagery tasks have been used to establish a simple form of yes/no communication with a few of his patients. This is done by asking them to imagine one activity (e.g. playing tennis), if the answer they wish to convey is yes. If the answer they wish to convey is no, he asks them to imagine a different activity (e.g. navigating around their house). This yes/no communication with a person who has a disorder of consciousness is, of course, rudimentary but still a breakthrough.

Death is nothing but withdrawal of consciousness from this body so that it can go elsewhere. The Upanishads equate human existence to a tree. We all are hollow and empty from inside, and are covered by the body like the trunk of the tree; the branches are the knowledge, which we gain through reading the scriptures, and by being in the presence of learned ones. Our thoughts and feelings are like the leaves which shake with the forces of nature (maya), they drop with time and new ones come out. We bear the fruits of our action but should never aspire to enjoy them ourselves as these fruits are for the passers-by who come underneath the tree to enjoy the fruit as well as the shade (our wisdom). Death is like the monkey who descends on the tree to drop the last seed so that the consciousness in you can be transferred to another tree or a soul.

So accept that the monkey will always be there. When we have reached maturity, every year the tree will bear seeds (our progeny), but one fine day the last seed will fall and we will be gone. Let us not be attached to the seed because this tree of ours came from another seed. Death is the most natural thing that happens to each and every aspect of this creation. Let us not be attached to the trunk, the branches, the leaves, the fruit or the seeds.

At the end of this chapter I would like to conclude by offering the depth of the very knowledge and the wonderful secret; the truth that is described in the holy Vedanta scriptures of the Upanishads, the Bhagavad Gita and the Vedas. Tell yourself: I am the Divine, the Emptiness, and the Infinite, and the Infinite, the Emptiness, The Divine is in me. At a macroscopic and microscopic level it is just the same. Everything that we perceive, feel, see, read is nothing but an illusion. Accept that you yourself are omnipotent and full of joy, and yet you are empty. Fathom this, constantly reflect on this, accept it, and all the miseries and bondage of the repeated cycle of birth and death, which you think you have, will disappear. Any fears that you have will dissipate. Revel in this truth and literally open your sense organs with the knowledge, to appreciate creation. The moment you accept this completely, your thoughts, emotions, and actions will change and you will get enlightened.

CHAPTER 6. Psychosis

WE ARE LIVING IN THIS WORLD, WHICH ACCORDING TO VEDANTA, itself is illusionary. But we breathe, talk, walk, and perform all the necessary functions to live. That cannot be denied. When the great seers teach that this world is illusionary, they invite us not to get too attached to things that have been provided to us by the Divine. One of the main reasons people become psychotic, or literally lose touch with reality, is because they become so attached to worldly items that they cannot see otherwise.

As growing children we slowly start recognizing that things are not necessarily always there forever. When we are just a few months old if a toy disappears (because it has fallen off the bed), we become full of despair and we cry. We think that it has gone. Mom comes running to us and as soon as the toy is delivered back to us we stop crying.

The only thing constant to a young child seems to be mother. A child might think: *She is always there to feed me, clean me, wash me. I need only to look into her eyes and I get the constant reassurance.* And mothers love to talk to their children because they feel such a deep, human connection, which can only be considered unadulterated love for the Divine. The Divinity, which shines through the eyes of a young child, beckons the mom to pour out her own love because it is so innocent, so joyful.

Now imagine yourself being so attached to the child that you do not want to let go of it. You literally want to swallow the child because it is so beautiful. A mother can have such a fantasy, but quickly recognizes that such thoughts are foolish and brushes them aside.

Let us take it a step further: the child feels rejected by the mother because the mother has gone through some sort of trauma and cannot bring herself to meet all the needs of the child. The child looks towards the mother and sees an empty, vacant look. He starts to doubt whether it is a safe place to live or not. He retreats into himself, feeling scared and unworthy. The child grows up and becomes a bit suspicious, and he does not know why. He is just waiting for the worst possible thing to happen to him. A psychotherapist can spend hours, months, or even years trying to help the adult understand how a deprived childhood can affect a person. But, in my experience, the child's sense of self worth never comes back adequately; rather the psychotherapist might suggest to the grownup child that he can blame the mother as she was never around him. So it is not his fault. We can imagine what the repercussions of that approach could be with regards to the mother-child relationship. Additionally, using this approach will not even answer the question as to why the mother was not there for him. His guilt for not being a good-enough child might always haunt him and make him feel scared and paranoid in this world.

This brings us along to the concept of karma – a concept easy to understand but easily misunderstood.

1. There is a reason for everything in this world.
2. Every action has an equal and opposite reaction.

Most people understand these two concepts: but let us try to examine their deeper meanings. The laws of the universe are pretty straightforward. Every particle of creation has been provided with its own karma. The reason that the rock is there is because it is there; a collection of minerals and other substances that make it the way it looks, feels, and behaves. Various forces inside the planet including sedimentation, heat, and air created it. The rock sits on the ground waiting for wind to continually blow and grind it down or for the human being to come along and break it down so that it can become a part of somebody's home. It has its role in this creation: and that is its karma.

As the most evolved species on the planet we likely have more karma than a simple rock. The Vedic seers described three different types of karma for each and every aspect of this creation.

1. *Sanchita karma,* or the karma over which we have no control. It is pre-ordained or pre-destined. Such a karma includes conditions such as where we were born, what city our parents were living in, who our parents were, who are our sibling/s, or other relatives. We do not have any control over any of these factors. Hence the seers decided that our past karma or impressions from previous lives dictate our sanchita karma.

2. Then there is *Prarabdha karma,* which is karma happening right now, at this very moment. So, taking the analogy of my interest in drinking a glass of beer, I have had previous exposure to drinking beer and hence I have laid down previous impressions on my mind (sanchita karma), and I am now drinking the beer (prarabdha karma), which is going to make a me bit tipsy and inebriated (agaami karma).

3. *Agaami karma* is the karma that is going to happen in the future based on our current actions.

To put it simply, the past dictates the present as well as the future. Sadly, people have taken this to literally mean that we have no control over the past and that our present and the future are pre-ordained. Thus we cannot modify our karma. But that is not what is implied here.

We can make a difference to our present right now. Going back to our example, my intellect is strong enough to allow me to appreciate that the glass of beer is just an object of my desire. I can chose to either ignore the urge invigorated by my senses or I can succumb to my desire to drink that glass of beer. The choice is indeed mine and I am shaping my karma accordingly. My action now will have an appropriate reaction in the future, which will further shape subsequent karmas.

Now, going back to the person whose mother was not available to him during his childhood. It was his sanchita karma that he was born in a house where his mother was unavailable. It would be his previous karmas (likely from a different lifetime) that made him be born in that home and have her as his mother. So he could not have controlled/modified what was going on with him at that time. But it is very much up to him now, in the present, to accept that it happened. You can control your present and your future. Every act that you are doing now shapes your future. Consequently, even though he may feel a bit suspicious of the world, he will benefit from the reality that this world is not a horrible place to live in. It was neither his mom's fault for not being there for him at such a young age, nor was it his fault that he feels the way he does. By practicing various spiritual techniques like prayer, meditation, and breathing exercises, which bring us closer to the Divine, we can shape our present and future.

History is replete with stories of great leaders being formed from people who have had deprived childhoods. Having faith helps us overcome our deficiencies and we are able to make a difference to ourselves and to humanity. If our potential is limitless then let us not worry about the past and be contented about the present, so that we will not be apprehensive about the future. Just live life fully now, feel wholesome and life will become purposeful. Enjoy every moment that the Divine has provided to us; the air that He gave us to breathe, the food to nourish us, the clothes to wear, and places to live. Count your blessings every moment and the anxieties just leave you.

A useful spiritual context with regards to the understanding of psychosis is that people have perceptual experiences different from others only because that they have a different reality. If we were to accept that this whole world is an illusion, can it not be extrapolated that some people (having psychotic experiences) are able to perceive this world slightly differently than others?

Just the other day I had a person come into my office for follow-up. She had been given a diagnosis of schizophrenia a very long time ago. She hears voices, has visual hallucinations, and has premonitions of her own death as well as those of some murdered people whose bodies will be thrown at the bottom of a ditch on a country road. Interestingly, she has been on various antipsychotics but there has been no improvement in any of her symptoms for more than thirty years. I tried to wear a spiritual hat that day in trying to really understand her experiences. I was so surprised when I heard her story from her point of view.

I learned a great deal from her. She shared that she believes that there is a spiritual reason for her experiences. Jesus is present everywhere and gives her special messages to help keep her safe. He sometimes comes to her in a blinding light and at other times takes the shape of various people warning her of bad things to come. She has never felt scared by these experiences. Even if Satan has tried to trouble her, the "Holy Light" has kept her safe. For her, these premonitions are her direct communication with the other world. The voices are the attempt of other souls in other worlds to talk to her.

This is an account of just one patient to whom I tried to really listen. Just imagine how many other people might be having similar experiences who are all labelled as schizophrenics, while they are just special people.

So far I had been listening to this woman's psychiatric symptoms, waiting for her to tell me more "bizarre" stuff. In this process I had kept her label of schizophrenia and had distanced myself from her. On reflection, I can only imagine the disservice that we do people who are so special when all a psychiatrist does is label this person with a diagnosis and "try" to treat them. Nobody believes their stories and they feel alienated in this world.

If we were to take her experiences as someone who was still able to keep the ego intact and consequently was able to communicate with us living in this reality; it is not too difficult to also imagine that when the ego is completely dissolved and presents as severe psychosis with thought dissolution, catatonia, and command hallucinations, then the mind and intellect have likely merged with the Supreme Consciousness. Some people are not able to differentiate this reality in which we all live from another reality. We, living in this reality, cannot even fathom what this other reality might look like. It unnerves us to even think that there could be another reality.

However, we do like to watch science fiction movies where we travel in space and meet aliens!

In the book called *Vasistha's Yoga* as explained by Swami Venkatesananda, there are beautiful treatises of an enlightened sage, Vasistha. This sage helps Lord Rama, one of the most benevolent and beautiful souls, gain his own enlightenment. I have read only the first few chapters of this book so far and I have been struck by its beautiful knowledge. I am so excited to have been given this book by a noble person, as a gift. Surely it will help me tremendously in my own journey as a seeker.

Sage Vasistha explains to Lord Rama that this whole world is an illusion. Each aspect of life that we see, be it the five elements which created the universe, or our bodies, minds, and intellects, the sensations that are perceived by all our sense organs are all an illusion. The source of sentiency or life is our *Atma*, or the Supreme Soul, or the Self, which resides in the seen and the unseen. It is what makes all of us live. This Atma gets tainted by our experiences of past lives, the misdemeanours of our current lives and our egos. We get stuck in the repeated cycles of birth and death; of wishes and wants and our inability to foresee our true Self being present everywhere.

The Sage also mentions, in his enlightened experience, that there are at least fourteen other universes, which the Divine has created. Isn't it interesting that from the time of Albert Einstein and subsequently, many physicists have now refined string theory, which acknowledges that there are at least ten other parallel universes? Perhaps a refinement in the string theory in the future might reveal even fourteen parallel universes!

Does the knowledge above not beg us to literally open our eyes, get enlightened, and consider the person who has different experiences than us to also have a right to have a different reality? Perhaps his reality is truer than ours. Blessed are those who can accept someone with psychosis as nothing more than an aberration of this creation. We all shun too much of a difference between one another. And we label the person who is experiencing a different world as "mad."

We human beings are likely our own worst enemies. There are a number of people who hear voices. This is a fact. Does that make them different from the rest of us? Why do we have such a stigma attached to interacting with people who "behave" a little bit differently than the rest, especially in terms of their mental health? The impressions of society make us "behave" toward and think of them as separate human beings. If we can show compassion for a person living with a form of cancer, why do we not show similar, if not more, compassion for a person who hears voices? It is not the person's "fault" that he hears voices. He is just living out his karmas; like we are living ours based on our past experiences. The Divine has made problems so that we can appreciate goodness too. The whole world is completely full of contrasts. With our intellect we have to appreciate that some people hear voices while others don't. Some people have cancers while others don't. Let us just accept our differences as a way of the Divine teaching us that though we may look, feel, think, and behave differently we still are one. The breath that we take is being dictated by the Self, which makes us live. Can I die just by holding my breath? NO. He offered us so many beautiful things to enjoy in this world, so let us just do those. Let us find bliss in every moment of our lives and the world will seem a wonderful place.

Think about yourself as a bubble in an ocean – just one single bubble. There are innumerable other bubbles in the ocean. We are all bobbing up and down, being generated and destroyed every moment. The ocean is the provider, the Divine, the fathomless, the infinite. We are so small yet so big. We are generated from the ocean and we go back into the ocean of the Divine. Such a simple message, yet so powerful.

CHAPTER 7. Obsessions and Compulsions

I HAVE A SET OF NEWTON BALLS IN MY OFFICE. I LOOK AT THEM every day as a reminder of a very basic law of nature: Every action has an equal and opposite reaction. If my mind has a negative thought, a bad thought, which could lead me to perform a negative action; I will have to complete a reaction (a compulsion) to get the bad thought out. For example, if I think I am dirty somehow, this could be because of a past experience of being violated or abused, or even something more subtle, which made my faith in humanity suffer. This might make me feel that I need to wash off this feeling of dirt that has crept into me. This would be a psychodynamic construct of how obsessions or compulsions are understood by psychiatrists and psychologists. Trying to explain this to a person who is suffering an illness usually leads us nowhere and hence we try to do behavioural experiments of various types. For example, we might expose and desensitise the person's thought process by showing him that there is actually nothing dirty on a tap or a hand and asking him to touch the "dirty" tap or hand. This is done in a completely safe manner in the presence of the therapist. Such behavioural therapies do usually work, but not for too long before a relapse occurs. This is likely because such therapies do not necessarily answer the reason of why the bad thought came in the first place. The person's underlying schemas or thought processes remain unchallenged and have not been adequately tackled.

Spiritual thinking allows us to go much deeper into understanding why obsessions and compulsions arise in the first place. First of all we need to accept that obsessions are natural and lots of people have them. It is not a weakness of the person who has them but just a weakness of the mind, which is not listening to the stronger intellect. An obsession arises when we let doubt take over our thinking processes. Our mind is nothing but a constellation of thoughts; they come and go. Some thoughts stick a little bit longer than others. The ones that are negative tend to stick a little bit longer, that is all. But our intellects are usually able to deflate/distract these negative thoughts as we recognize that there is no basis for them. We use logic and past experience to annul such foolish thoughts. If so, I might have a doubt that the tap is dirty but even so, I am not going to touch it with my bare hands. I am going to use a clean Kleenex to open the tap instead. My intellect is telling me that this idea is stupid and foolish but because my doubt sometimes feels so strong, I just succumb and let it take over me and therefore do use the Kleenex.

However obsessions do not always win, that is also a fact. I have not met one person with a diagnosis of Obsessive Compulsive Disorder who has not been able to win over their obsession at some time. They have all recognized that their thoughts are silly, but the power of the thought processes can be so strong that people sometimes feel they have no option but to bend.

If we were to now examine obsessive-compulsive thought processes spiritually – the whole world is full of billions of people having many billions and billions of thoughts every second. If everyone listened to each and every thought, then it would be impossible to live in this beautiful world. The nature of a thought is to come and go. However, the intellect is what is connected to the Supreme Energy, the Divinity, which made us have these thoughts in the first place. If we start having more and more faith in the Divine, lower thought processes like obsessions and compulsive acts just wither away. They have no option but to do so. If we were to follow the various spiritual practices, as described previously, they will help tremendously in letting go of the obsessive thoughts as well as compulsive actions.

From my so-far limited experience, I have seen some people who do get stuck with a number of obsessive thoughts. They do not have faith in themselves and as a result, trying to find faith in the Divine is even more difficult for them. Additionally, some people might have had a bad experience in a religious setting while young and now they might struggle to find faith in God. When I see such people in clinic, I say to them: Do not fret. Faith is one thing which grows, albeit slowly. Try and find good things in yourself before you start questioning the actions of others or of the Divine. The very fact that you are alive at the moment means that the Divine wishes you to be alive to be breathing this air that He has provided. Start feeling grateful for everything that you come across. Every experience that you have, good or bad, is an expression of the joy that the Divine has provided. Accept that as His grace and let tears of compassion flow through you. Faith takes away obsessive doubt. Pray and meditate on the Self without any prejudices of the past or worries about the future. The Divine is here all the time, was there before you were born, and will continue to be there after you are dead. You are a small person in the sea of humanity, yet you are the Divine too. The light of the Divine is shining inside you, but might have been covered by various layers of our thoughts, emotions, prejudices, ego, and memories. The Divine is supremely powerful. These layers have to be slowly unfolded by the person himself as a seeker.

Just breathe the air that the Divine has provided and be thankful for Him allowing you to be alive. Live in the present moment listening, feeling, hearing, and seeing every aspect of this beautiful creation that is there for you. Close your eyes and feel the warmth and the glow of your breath as it goes in and out. Feel the energy go in with you every time that you breathe in and let every exhalation make you feel calm and relaxed. When a bad thought comes into your head, when you are meditating or when you have your eyes open, just examine the thought as just a fantasy; something which your mind created, though you are so much more than your thoughts. YOU ARE THE SELF. Let that thought grow in you and you will feel deeper and more powerful breaths invigorate your body. The energy of the Divine will feel stronger. Continue to do other spiritual practices including seva towards others, and slowly your faith will grow.

When you do find yourself feeling on some days that your faith is weak, and such days will happen, don't blame yourself or the Divine, for not being able to maintain the faith at that moment. Faith grows as we let it grow. Each and every positive experience that we have needs to be acknowledged and offered back to the Divine in complete gratitude. The obsessive, doubtful thoughts and compulsive reactions then just slowly dissolve away. Keep the faith and keep performing your practices.

I would now like us to examine symmetry in nature. Have you not noticed that this reality is nothing but a complex array of objects, which are laid out in perfect sequence? Everything is symmetrical. Let us start with our own bodies. Just about everything is symmetrical at a macro as well as micro level. The left hand is symmetrical to the right. The left foot is symmetrical to the right. Our navel is in the centre of this symmetrical body. Through the navel we were connected to our mother's womb, which provided us with life-giving nourishment. The same life-line is the Divine showering its love on us through provision of energy, vitamins, minerals and the energy that powers us now in our adult lives. As we started to grow, we became impressed by the way nature expresses everything in symmetry too. The tiniest animal to the most exquisite plant has symmetry. The snowflake might look crooked but if you examine it in a microscope the crystals are perfectly aligned. Even within each human or any other living cell, the DNA is nothing but nucleic acids bound to each other in complete symmetry. As we go deeper into the level of atoms, which make up the nucleic acids, that is the carbon, hydrogen and oxygen (and others which form the periodic table), all atoms are completely symmetrical.

We are also faced with a great deal of asymmetry in life. Nothing seems to be in order. Everywhere we look there is chaos. Nothing seems to be predictable with our emotions or our thoughts. When we look at the way people behave we just cannot seem to understand why they behave the way they do. Why is there anarchy in some parts of the world, while in other parts there is relative calm? Why are there cycles of calm and political eruptions? Why does the stock market behave so unpredictably? The financial pundits might want to make us believe that there is only one way for a stock to go; i.e. up, but we also know that the stock goes down very frequently and unpredictably. People are born and they die. So yes, there is much unpredictability in this world. Even at a micro level, as quantum mechanics is now showing us, there is complete unpredictability of quarks, boson, and other articles being produced and destroyed.

So there seems to be a simple story emerging. The truth is that this world is nothing but organized chaos. Symmetry and Asymmetry seem to run together everywhere that we look. The truth, at a deeper level is, that the Divine created us all, and he wishes us to appreciate this. We see the duality like happy and sad thoughts, good and evil, hot and cold. This duality is in the external real world that we can see and is always changing. But underneath all of this reality is a substratum on which the dance of change is happening. Hence everything is just one. The eternal. The only truth. There is only one Brahman, or the eternal Self, that is present in you, me, and everything around us.

Let me now also share some of my personal reflections on the subject of obsessions and compulsions. I recognize that there could be advantages to having obsessions and compulsions too. Don't we sometimes all hate change? Everywhere and everything that you look is changing, and we ask ourselves on some days why we have to change. Let things remain the way they are.

But at another level we like change too. We don't want to be doing the same things repeatedly. We don't want to drive the same old car. We don't want to make the meals and do the dishes so many times, day in and day out. It gets so boring.

So our minds get confused, it questions why there is so much change, versus, whether there's a need for change. The only escape that it finds at times is to repeat things. Likely our minds feel more settled with obsessive habits and thoughts. These habits negate change and put our minds to rest. We feel less awful and more comfortable in our own selves, facing the change.

Now comes another secret revelation.

Through certain types of meditation we can all go into a deep state of relaxation where we come to know of our true natures. Such forms of meditation require repeated use of a particular mantra or *japa* to help the mind focus, concentrate, and listen to the intellect. The frequent use of the mantra helps the person tune into the substratum consciousness. The repeated, if not obsessive, use of the mantra helps us to let go of our attachment to this materialistic world and the mind becomes still and calm.

You would have noticed that there is a strange phenomenon in this world. Before any stillness we frequently notice a sort of an agitation. For example, after any storm there is always a strange stillness. Similarly, stirring up the mind with a mantra or japa to get slightly agitated is a scientific way to reach the deeper state of relaxation. When a meditator reaches the calmness, he escapes into a world where everything is still; where three dimensions of space do not exist, time does not exist, emotions do not exist, and thoughts do not exist. We feel as if we are completely hollow inside. It is so beautiful and exquisite that words cannot even describe it.

Experienced meditators always have smiles on their faces because they can just be with this changeless reality. They recognize that everything that their sense organs are perceiving, that the mind is feeling, that their intellects are thinking; is changing. However, the sub-stratum, the Divine force, which provides the energy is constant. So let us just reflect on this and the Divinity will guide us.

All the learned people have implored us to seek discipline in our daily lives so that we can bring our undisciplined minds to meditate. That is the truth. However, the other truth is also that when you go into a higher state of knowing, discipline is no longer needed. The Self starts to work its magic through you. Your gut starts to talk to you. Your intuition develops. You are able to see through the symmetry and the asymmetry. You constantly marvel at the Lord's creation and revel in being alive. You start to have constant love for the Creator.

So, o seeker, if you are troubled with obsessional thoughts and compulsive actions, recognize that your mind is trying to make sense of this reality.

All you have to do is to let go of your preconceived ideas about why there is dirt that you need to clean, or that things have to be put in a right place. Recognise that symmetry and asymmetry go together; that cleanliness and dirt go together. They are just two sides of the same coin of this reality. Reflect on this truth, find a Divine soul who can help you meditate, and let go of these thoughts. Immerse yourself in loving the Creator and all your obsessions and compulsions will just wither away. That is guaranteed. Have faith.

And when our minds talk too much, our mouths also talk. Respecting silence is one of the most important spiritual techniques that we can learn. When we become experienced meditators we find silence and bliss in the quietness. In this active rajasic world, finding silence in the midst of all the chatter becomes even more important. We are also frequently stuck with feelings of tamas or inertia, where we really do not want to do anything but our minds are agitated. When we are in silence there is a rise in our level of intuition and energy. Just admire creation when you are silent. We don't need to speak every time that we hear something.

When my mind is constantly abuzz I have learnt a wonderful technique. Do try it out. I just go out and admire one aspect of creation. You could look up towards the sky, straight up, so that you cannot see the horizon. You will feel so small and insignificant. Indeed that is what we are; just small specks of matter and energy in this creation. So our troubling thoughts are even smaller in this creation. Our obsessive ruminations are even smaller. They have no option but to go away when we respect the creation. Just feel the stress leave you in just a few seconds. And try to remain in this feeling of bliss when you go back to what you were doing. Obsessions will have no option but to recede when we are in the blissful state.

Our current environment prompts us to speak and respond every time. But ask any psychiatrist or psychologist and they will tell you that the most talking happens when we are silent. Our bodies and minds speak so well to each other through silence. As we practice patience and silence, slowly we feel less need to speak anyway. When words come out they will have more meaning and will be for the greater good of humanity. All the great saints have also said to speak less and do more. Finding the time to do more without any prejudices or expectations leads the mind to become even quieter. One of the common psychological techniques that we tend to use frequently is distraction. It is just this. If the mind has a tendency to talk, let us use it more productively. The activity that we do makes our mind focused on the job and the obsessive thoughts just go away. If that activity is directed towards something positive for someone else, then the positive karma comes back to you even more. You will find silence far more invigorating when you meditate next time. So learn to do more seva by being involved in activities for others, all the time. Your ego will be defeated and you will feel more relaxed and empowered to do more.

I constantly hear from people that they cannot find an activity to engage in. The likely cause of such a claim is because we have become so self-obsessed that we do not get out of our homes. The most tiresome activity is loneliness. We need to have an intention of removing our loneliness by making one phone call/email/Facetime/Facebook/Twitter to a different person every day. Any person on the path knows that they cannot keep happiness or sadness to themselves. Even if you are an introvert, you will find an activity that really will make you feel relaxed. You know what that is going to be. Don't let your ego and your past experience dictate to your mind that there is nothing out there to take you out of your loneliness. Even if you have lost a loved one and you are in grief and despair, even at that stage it becomes all the more important to find something to do for someone. It will let your mind heal so more quickly.

CHAPTER 8. Post-Traumatic Stress Disorder

LET US START THIS CHAPTER BY ACCEPTING THE FACT THAT IN THIS world no one person has had the exact experiences as another or is the same personality as another. We know that even twins, who might share similar DNA do not have the same experiences. They therefore see this world in a different light and turn out to have different personalities. Hence, everyone in this creation is unique. As we start to let go of our egos through our awakening, we will become much more in tune with ourselves and celebrate our differences and the uniqueness of everyone around us.

Now let us try to understand from the spiritual point of view, the foundation of the mental state that is commonly labelled as Post-Traumatic Stress Disorder (PTSD). What we have now become, the way that we think and behave, is based on our experiences, which shape our memories, egos, and our belief systems. Some of us will consider our childhoods made of mostly happy memories while others might not be that "lucky" and may have been hurt or even abused. So my experience might have shaped a particular memory, including being abused in some way, and hence it is expected that my emotions and my mind will be affected by such experiences. My mind, like any human being's, is by nature weak. If I have faced something dreadful, an abuse or a calamity of some sort, it is but natural for me to fear for my safety; to feel threatened that my whole world is going to come crashing down on me; that I have to live in a constant fear and my only thought and recourse is to avoid the situation that led me to be abused or hurt. I might have very vivid memories and even flashbacks of the abusive situations.

Whenever or wherever there is a trigger in the environment, which leads to rekindling of our memories by an image, a sound, a smell, or even taste of something, our sense organs react immediately. The mind goes into overdrive trying to save the body, mind, and intellect equipment from any potential danger. We start having short shallow breaths similar to when we feel anxious. Our minds shuts down in panic and we dread that the hurtful situation might begin again.

We have previously learnt that our innate Self is infinite and calm as well as joyful. But if our memories and ego equipment have been affected by an abusive insult, the Self is covered by the body-defence systems and is unable to express itself through the intellect. If a person has to get out of a repetitive cycle of avoidance, flashbacks, nightmares, and hyper-arousal, he might have to resort to a spiritual technique to calm the body. There is now a lot of research to show that specific breathing techniques called sudarshan kriya yoga help us in coming out of PTSD symptoms with ease and without any effort. The body's stress levels, as measured by serum cortisol and blood immune markers, also show an improvement. The person does not feel triggered that easily even in the presence of the triggering stimuli.

How sudarshan kriya works in PTSD is not yet very well understood but there is a suspicion that the change in the breath forces a sympathetic withdrawal and resetting of the parasympathetic tone from the brain and the spinal cord. What this means is that the heart slows down so that the mind does not interpret the environment as being threatening. As a result, the memory is not triggered, and the body feels less tense and then relaxes through meditation.

There is enough research to prove that sudarshan kriya yoga works in people who have been exposed to acute distress after an environmental disaster such as the Tsunami in Southeast Asia in 2004, as well as in people exposed to conflict through war. I am now interested in exploring the benefits of this technique in a routine psychiatry clinic where people present with PTSD symptoms after exposure to various sorts of acute and chronic abusive and threatening situations. We shall be starting a pilot study in the next few months.

The modulation of the breath by sudarshan kriya yoga is likely one of the most effective behavioural aspects of Vedanta for controlling symptoms of PTSD. Now let us also consider the intellectual basis of Vedanta and its benefits for PTSD. As we have uncovered so far, this whole world and creation is unreal due to the influence of maya. So if I were to let go of the thought that I am guilty for the way that I experienced an abusive situation, that it was only maya that presented itself as that situation, I might be able to face the present and the future much more easily.

We have also read that our experiences are to some extent shaped by our karmas. But I can reshape my future, by steps that I take now. The past does not define the present or the future. If my true nature is the Infinite, then how is it possible that my past experiences will dictate my present or the future? By plain logic itself, that is impossible to comprehend.

Let me repose myself in this truth; that my nature is Love and the Divine. I am neither a victim nor a sufferer. These are labels that people have put on me so that I feel comforted in receiving the help that people wish to provide me. I am more than a label. I am the infinite whose past has no bearing on my current self. My natural state in this heavenly body is a relaxed state. By learning how to breathe properly, I can and I will make my body learn that the past is over and it has no control over my present moment. I can and I will define my present and future.

If I focus on my breath during kriya and meditation I will learn of my true inner self, which is calm, relaxed, simple, and empty. There are no memories there. It is safe there. Not because it is a cocoon, but because the emptiness is what defines me. I am infinite. The infinite is not defined by time or experiences. Let me take a deep breath in. The breath will provide me with the energy to face the world and look at it in an accepting light.

I will then take a long breath out which will make me so relaxed that the hyper-arousal states, the flashbacks and the nightmares will simply recede.

Let me repose myself in this knowledge and this illness will just leave me. I have the faith.

CHAPTER 9. Alcohol, Gambling, and Addictions

I KNOW THAT YOU KNOW OF AT LEAST ONE INDIVIDUAL WHO HAS tried gambling, alcohol, tobacco, or other inebriants, intoxicants, and stimulants and felt adversely affected by them. Heroin, cocaine, cannabis, LSD and other drugs can cause physical and psychological dependence. These are such powerful agents that even though our intellects dissuade us from using them, we feel strongly pulled by our need and desire to consume them again and again. They do provide pleasure, that is a given. We also know they can cause a lot of grief for our loved ones and ourselves; that is also a given.

If you know that their usage has become a habit, then that is the first step to recognize that something needs to change.

Psychiatrists, counsellors, and psychologists have traditionally used harm-reduction strategies, Alcoholics Anonymous (AA), and Gamblers Anonymous (GA), as well as other group-based psychological interventions to help someone whose life has been adversely affected by these addictions. Such techniques seem to reduce the extent of problems associated with these various addictions. However, time and again it has been shown that people affected by addictions are not able to come off these agents for any significant period of time and they frequently relapse.

I am not going to describe the cycle of change, which AA uses, because inevitably if you have had a problem with alcohol, you have been either referred to or have been a user of AA and you know it works to some extent. I am also not going to describe about the changes happening in the brain, which have biologically shown why people feel so helpless under the influence of addictive agents.

In the rest of this chapter I will attempt to provide a simpler understanding of how we can get rid of addictions by using spiritual concepts as provided by Vedanta.

Let me tell you another story. You might have heard a few in your lifetime; of successes and/or failures of people trying to come off addictive agents. Here is one from my family.

My grandfather was a chain smoker for a long time. He used to smoke cigarettes as well a pipe. When I was young I remember seeing him with his hands always stained brown. He smelt awful with the smell that one gets from someone who smokes a lot regularly. His whole home used to be reeking of tobacco smoke. Additionally he had a chronic cough.

As a child, every summer I would go with my family to be with him and my grandmother. His smoking habit was the only thing that I despised. He made the best rice *pulao* and was extremely caring. We would get candies every day when we went out with him, and he ordered fresh *samosas* in the evening. He loved dogs as pets and he used to love to entertain his grandkids. But the smoking seemed to go on every year that we visited him. But on one of our summer breaks, I noticed that he did not have his customary pack of cigarettes and lights in his coat pocket. He looked a bit sullen and grumpy, though that was nothing unusual for him. Still, I was wonderfully surprised that he had no cigarette in his hand! I was curious and I asked him if he had stopped smoking. I must have been between ten and eleven years old. I remember him saying very gruffly, "She made me stop," pointing towards my grandmother. He would not elaborate. Later I came to know that my grandmother had given him an ultimatum. That was it. He had to stop. And so he did.

He relapsed a few times. But every time, she was there to support him and cajole him. Whatever her technique was, it worked. For thirty plus years after that, he did not smoke. He died recently. And he never had angina, a heart attack, stroke, or lung disease. Thankfully the physical effects of the smoke dissipated. He was peaceful when he passed away.

So let us look at this story from a spiritual point of view. First, let us accept that addiction has become a problem for us. Denial will not take us forward. It is our past impressions or karma that made us develop such habits in the first place. But, with the right and firm intention we can let go of our old karma. Our new positive actions will give us positive results. So blaming our karma for inaction and getting stuck in the habit does not help us.

Second, learn that nobody is going to help you as much as you can yourself. There are wonderful spiritual practices that can help you in the process. Following such practices help increase our resolve to come off these addictive agents. Yoga and meditation have consistently helped people to come off all addictive habits. You just have to be unfailing in your practices to find the benefit from them.

Yoga, by definition, means bringing the body, the mind, and the intellect together. As mentioned before, yoga is not only about asanas that we practice but is also the magnificent knowledge of how we can learn to train the mind. There are a few treatises and scriptures written in ancient India about how yoga is best practiced. They are priceless. Try and find a master who will help you discover the wonderful knowledge of yoga.

Third, implore yourself to find the love for this knowledge. This could be Divine love, or for dear ones like your sibling, your parents, or your guru. With the promise that you give your dear ones, your intention becomes stronger, and your resolve becomes unwavering.

If the above does not work, try a couple of other strategies. Be greedy in your intention. Say to yourself that if you do not fall prey to these addictive agents, you will be rewarded by something. Of course this can be your fantasy. If you are lucky it might even come true. Think that you are going to win a lottery, that you will never fall sick, that you will be extremely successful. Think of something that is close to your heart and provides a positive feeling, just by thinking of it.

If this does not work, think of something that will instil some fear in your mind. We all are fearful of something or other. I have not met anyone who has no fears unless they are enlightened. And such enlightened people are not affected by many of the problems that we seekers have to traverse through. Think that if you were to again succumb to your addiction, great misery would befall you. This could be having a serious illness, losing your assets, or having something bad happen to your loved ones. Bring this thought again and again when your mind and body quiver for the addictive agent. Either of the above two techniques will work, depending on your innate style of motivation and/or inspiration.

At this stage I would also like to discuss a little bit about why we have habits. We indeed all are creatures of habit. I know that when I need to sit at the dining table I will choose a particular chair that I like to sit on. Each person in the family also has a favourite chair. Don't we observe that at each stage of our lives, be it childhood, adulthood, or middle age we all are stuck with habits. Why do we get these habits? What is the purpose of habits?

If we try to find the answer on a spiritual basis, the way of letting go of habits lies in finding enlightenment. If you feel that you are more than your habit, that you want to let go of your habits, then you should feel blessed that you wish to let go of the bondage that keeps you in this materialistic world again and again. The only way for us to stop our habits completely is to find enlightenment. Then only will we be able to get rid of the repeated cycle of birth and death. *Ashtavakra*, a great sage in India, who was born more than 5000 years ago, said that the sole purpose of life, the only reason we are living right now, is to find enlightenment. All our desires arise from the sense organs, and with each desire we get stuck. We like to eat particular foods (to satisfy our desire to taste and smell something pleasant). We wear particular clothes (to fulfil our desire of seeing something appealing). We listen to certain types of music (to satisfy our hearing), and have sex (to satisfy touch). These all become habits and we get stuck because of these habits. Each time that we succumb to our habits, new impressions (*vasanas*) are being laid in our mind and the cycle repeats itself. We are more than our sense organs, our habits and our *vasanas*. These habits are only there to serve as a constant reminder that we have to look inwards to find our very true nature. The Divine put habits in us so that we can appreciate our true nature by letting go of them. Let us not feel enamoured of or even feel guilty about our habits. Let them not control us, but let us just let go of our habits by revelling in the knowledge available to us right now, so that we may become enlightened, right now.

This can be done through reflecting on just five principles of *Ashtavakra*. Some of these we have previously read about in this book. It will be worth recapitulating these and learning a few others.

Please note, that these qualities or jewels are present in each and every one of us. You do not have to work hard on them to make a special effort to integrate these values into your life. We all are blessed with them already. We only have to provide the right support for them to fully blossom.

The first jewel is forgiveness (*shama*), towards yourself, and everyone else. There is no need to hold a grudge, or anger against someone else or yourself. The Divine is ready to accept you as long as you forgive yourself. This creation is replete with stories of goons, thugs, and murderers who have found enlightenment just because they sought forgiveness for themselves from the Divine. We all have a habit of blaming others as well as ourselves for lies that they/we spoke, or for hurt that someone/we gave. Let us forgive and forget. By remaining stuck in the perceived guilt we are allowing the memory to linger, the ego to grow, and the difference between you and me to grow. Everybody needs just one "Aha" moment for him or her to realize his or her true nature. Then the journey begins.

Second, let us practice sincerity (*arjava*). We just need to be sincere to remain on the path of seeking enlightenment and the road will open up right away for us. Even if there are stumbling blocks on the path, we can accept them the way they are and try not to read too much into them. A correct frame of mind for someone who encounters obstacles is to consider the obstacles as Divine food or *prasad* that the Divine has given to us. The fact that you did not get what you desired, if it was a virtuous desire (rather than a vile one), was the Self showing you that you have to sculpt your work a bit more till it becomes perfect. Have we not worked hard at something and then received a wonderful sense of accomplishment when it is complete? That is all sincerity means. Continue at your project till your gut tells you that it is good enough, and then stop. If we are grateful for the prasad that we receive during every opportunity that we get in this world, our sincerity to find enlightenment grows.

Third, be compassionate (*daya*), towards others as well as ourselves. The more compassionate that we are, the more easily our true nature blossoms. Love everyone, including those who are ignorant or who do harm to others and to you. They need more of our compassion than the ones who are good-natured do. Don't just gossip about the people who are lethargic, or who do not do anything positive – rather try to find the Divine in these people. We need to maintain our constant feelings of compassion towards each and every one.

Fourth, be content (*santosh*), with what you have and don't aspire for more. As soon as compassion becomes our very nature, we become contented. Revel and keep faith in the knowledge that the Divine shall provide what we need. Why fret over spilled milk or worry about the future? Why be jealous of your neighbour or your colleague? They also have the same body, mind, and intellect equipment that you have. That is it. Let us revel in being members of humanity and part of this creation.

And finally, seek the truth (*satyam*). The only truth is that this world is changing on a substratum of the changeless. Realise this at every moment of your life. You are getting old and you will die. Nothing will be left behind. So be a witness of this creation and enjoy it. Let go of any preconceived ideas about what you need to do daily, or what the other person should do. Know that you are not the fire, the water, or the air, which you can see, feel, and perceive. You are but the changeless, the soul which is covered by a body, mind, and intellect (with additional layers of ego and memory). This is the truth.

SACRED CONVERSATIONS

As I end this book I would like to tell you one last story as described in Vasistha's Yoga. This story shows a wonderful conversation between an enlightened king called Vikram and an enlightened demon called Karkati, who threatened to devour the king if he replied wrongly to any of her questions. We gain wonderful insight into the concept of the Divine Self through their conversation, recognising that the Self is fathomable yet difficult to appreciate. That is the beauty of this wonderful knowledge. We are a part of this creation and we exist and so do other things, and we are all a part of it. That is it.

Karkati asks Vikram, "O King what is it that is one and yet is many, and in which millions of universes merge even as ripples in an ocean? What is it that is pure space, though it appears to be not so? What is it that is me in you and that is you in me? What is it that moves yet does not move – that remains stationary though it is not so. What is it that is as a rock, though conscious, and what plays wonderful tricks in empty space? What is it that is not the sun and the moon and fire and yet eternally shines? What is that atom that seems to be so far and yet so near? What is it that is of the nature of consciousness and yet is not knowable? What is it that is all and yet is not any of these? What is it that is the very Self of all, is veiled by ignorance, and is regained after many lifetimes of intense and persistent effort? What is it that is atomic and yet contains a mountain within it, and that transforms the three worlds into a blade of grass? What is it that is atomic and yet is immeasurable? What is it that without ever renouncing its atomic nature appears to be bigger than the biggest mountain? What is that atom in which the entire universe rests like a seed during the cosmic dissolution?

"O King, what is the Creator of this universe and by whose power do you exist and function as a king, protecting your subjects and punishing the wicked? What is it seeing which your own vision has purified and that you exist as alone, without a division? (This reference shows that Karkati was able to judge that Vikram was already enlightened even without him speaking a word yet.)

King Vikram replied, "I shall surely answer your questions. For that to which all your questions refer is the Supreme Self.

"That Self is subtler than space itself since it has no name and cannot be described, and neither the mind nor the senses can reach it or comprehend it. It is pure consciousness. The entire universe exists in the consciousness that is atomic, even as a tree exists within the seed, but then the universe exists as consciousness and does not exist as the universe. What we think is the universe exists for the pleasure of our sensations, but really does not exist. The sensations are illusory, this world is illusory, this body, mind, and intellect are also illusionary. What does exist is the consciousness. That consciousness exists, however, because such is the experience of all, and since it alone is the Self of all. Since it is, all else is.

"That Self is empty like space, but it is not nothingness, since it is consciousness, which by nature is infinite. Infinite cannot be fathomed or comprehended. It can only be accepted. It is. Yet because it cannot be experienced by the mind and senses, it is not. It being the Self of all, it is not experienced (as the object of experience) by anyone. Though one, it is reflected in the infinite items of existence and hence appears to be many. This appearance is, however, unreal even as a bracelet made of gold is an imaginary appearance of gold itself. The gold alone is real. But the Self is not unreal. It is not a void or nothingness, for it is the Self of all, and it is the very Self of one who says it is and of one who says (or thinks) it is not! Moreover, its existence can be experienced indirectly just as the existence of camphor can be experienced by its fragrance. It alone is the Self of all as consciousness, and it alone is the substance that makes the world's appearance possible.

In that infinite ocean of consciousness, whirlpools known as the three worlds (earth, heaven, and hell) arise spontaneously and naturally, even as whirlpools are caused by the very nature of running water. Because this consciousness is beyond the reach of the mind and senses, it seems to be a void. But since it can be known by self-knowledge, it is not a void. On account of the indivisibility of consciousness, I am you and you are me, but the indivisible consciousness itself has become neither I nor you! When the wrong notions of "you" and "I" are given up, there arises the awareness that there is neither you, nor I, nor everything; perhaps it alone is everything.

The Self, being infinite, moves not though moving, and yet it is forever established in every atom of existence (including in sub-atomic particles and the nothingness in-between). The Self does not go nor does it ever come, for space and time derive their meaning from consciousness alone. Where can the Self go when all that exists is within it? If a pot is taken from one place to another, the space within does not move from one place to another, for everything is forever in space.

The Self, which is of the nature of pure consciousness, seems to be inert and insentient when it is apparently associated with inertia. In infinite space, this infinite consciousness had made infinite objects appear. Though all this seems to have been done, because such an effect is a mere illusion, nothing has been done. Hence, it is both consciousness and inertia, the doer and the non-doer (reflecting the subjective experience of the experiencer and an objective experience of the observer).

The reality in fire is this Self or consciousness, yet, the self does not burn nor is it burnt, since it is the reality in all and is infinite. It is the eternal light, which shines in the sun, the moon, and the fire, but independent of them. It shines even when these have set, it illumines all from within all. It alone is that intelligence that dwells even in trees, plants, and creepers, and preserves them. That Self or infinite consciousness is, from the ordinary point of view, the creator, the protector, and the destroyer of all (equating to the Hindu Gods of Brahma, Vishnu, and Shiva), and yet from the absolute point of view, in reality, being the Self of all, it has no such limited rules. The Self is not a God residing in the heavens, or an entity which is outside of a sentient body, it is everywhere with energy that cannot be comprehended.

There is no world independent of this consciousness – even the mountains are in the atomic self. In it arise the fantasies of a moment and of an epoch, which appear to be real time-scales even as objects seen in the dream appear to be real at that time. Within the twinkling of an eye there exists an epoch, even as a whole city is reflected in a small mirror.

Such being the case, how can one assert the reality of either duality or non-duality? This atomic self or infinite consciousness alone appears to be a moment or an epoch, near and far, and there is nothing apart from it; and these are not mutually contradictory in themselves.

As long as one sees the bracelet as a bracelet, it is not seen as gold, but when it is seen that "bracelet" is just a word and not the reality, then gold is seen. Even so, when the world is assumed to be real, the self is not seen, but when this assumption is discarded, consciousness is realized. It is the all and therefore real. It is not experienced, and so it is unreal.

What appears to be is the jugglery of maya, which creates a division in consciousness into subject and object. It is as real as the dream-city. It is neither real nor unreal, but a long-standing illusion. It is the assumption of division that creates diversity, from the Creator right down to the little insect. Just as in a single seed the diverse characteristics of the trees remain at all times, this apparent diversity exists in the Self at all times, but as consciousness.

Last Thoughts

I WOULD LIKE TO END THIS BOOK BY SHARING SOME FINAL thoughts. I do not wish you, the reader, to somehow think that this writer has become enlightened. I am a seeker just like you. I still have pangs of psychological pain for no reason. Thoughts that are negative and demeaning still do affect me on some days. I have good days and bad days, just like you. I still cannot say that I am not dependent on another person's kind words to make me feel happy, cherished, and wanted. I still need to have my piece of chocolate in the evening to satisfy the lust of my tongue. I still enjoy putting my foot on the accelerator to get that wonderful feeling in my stomach, and I crave sex every few days. I am not enlightened.

However, things have changed tremendously. My moments of feeling despondent or anxious are negligible. I have a deeper and richer connection with everyone, including those in closest proximity; my wife and my children. My wife and I need to hash out things less than we used to, and we just accept. If my ego rises, she gently applies the brakes. If I have grown spiritually, it is only because she has been there behind me all the time, supporting me, and guiding me. I am indeed blessed to live in a household where the name of the Lord is now recited every day, where the adults meditate, and the children respect the name of the Lord. Where my wife and I are established and understand our roles and responsibilities. We are like the two vital energies running the household. She is the

mother, the Divine energy or the *Shakti*, which drives the kitchen, orches-
trates the calendar, and responds to the emotional and physical needs of
the children. I am the driver who steers the direction of the car of life.
I manage the finances, do the chores, and take the kids to their classes
and outdoor activities. We feel content with what we have and aspire for
nothing more.

I try not to run away from difficult situations. I feel connected even with
those whom I previously perceived as enemies. I can see through people's
motives and intentions better. I can smile outwardly easily, to make people
smile back. I am able to examine my thoughts more fully on most days.
When the feelings of despair and despondency do arrive I try to observe
them with a detached view, rather than blaming myself, the world, my
relationships, my past, or any crazy apprehensions about the future. I try
to laugh off that maya can be so strong that it is relentless in its pursuit of
keeping this mind stuck and the ego strong. As a seeker I do try to find the
knowledge in everything and everyone that I interact with.

Here is one last story and reflection. Last night I was not able to sleep too
well. As I transitioned from reflection, to contemplation, and finally to the
stillness that comes just before going off to sleep, I was suddenly jolted up
by my dear wife. Apparently I had been snoring! Such are the advantages
of a relaxed, meditative mind. You can go off to sleep quickly but sadly
the epiglottis at the back of your throat also enjoys the relaxation. It starts
to sing in tandem with your breath. Then the poor person next to you is
subjected to wonderful, and sometimes loud lullabies.

Having had only a few hours of sleep last night, I got up a bit heavy headed
this morning. I had no option but to retreat to my den in the basement
at 3:30 a.m. to read some knowledge and then try to meditate. As I was
sitting in my meditative position I could hear a rumbling noise. My cat
had now chosen to spend his sleeping time in my lap and was purring so
loudly that I just could not meditate. Karma, as my young daughter would
have said. I troubled my wife last night and now the cat was troubling me.

These two incidents also helped me further reflect. If our innate nature is
complete stillness, be it during the day, going off to sleep, in deep sleep or

in dreams, our biggest barrier to reach our nature still remains our egos. The ego makes us constantly aware that we are not enlightened yet. It sits on our head purring/snoring loudly and preventing us from being still. It's constantly reminding us that we have to let go of our egos to get to the state of full relaxation called enlightenment.

I am now sincere with my spiritual practices. I wake up early in the morning, read a scripture for ten minutes, then practice sudarshan kriya yoga for twenty minutes, and finally I meditate for around twenty minutes. After that I hit my emails and am able to work easily for twelve to fourteen hours without feeling tired. Gone are the days when I would feel tired in the middle of the day or dose off during conversations and meetings.

On days that I miss my spiritual practices for any reason, I feel out of touch with my Self. Meditation and kriya are like nectar to me, which provides calmness as well as invigorates this body and mind, especially on negative days. Hence, my request to you, o seeker, is that you be regular and disciplined with your spiritual practices, on your journey. I hope you find these practices as fulfilling as I have found them.

And lastly, I wish to share my interaction with someone whom I met yesterday. This event again, literally, opened my eyes. This person claimed that he was extremely happy in this world. He said he actually hated people who go onto the path of spirituality. He felt that people on the spiritual path become so dry and humourless that they are no longer able to function. He claimed that they put spirituality first and have withdrawn so much from this world that they are no longer taking part in its "enjoyable" activities. He felt that the person on the spiritual path needs to be aware of the importance of wealth, the materialistic advantage of gaining more power, the enjoyment in being able to get on the top based on personal achievement, and the feeling of strength that this gives. He had a personal account of a friend of his who had become "so sucked" into the spiritual path that he felt he had lost him. This friend had stopped coming to parties and no longer drank any alcohol. It seemed as if he talked only about spiritual things and was trying to force the rest of his friends to join the path. As a result, this person to whom I was talking, thoroughly hated spirituality and declared that he would "never ever" consider becoming a part of any such movement.

I was struck by the deep conviction that this man displayed. It also showed me that some sincere seekers might be taking this spiritual knowledge too seriously. At the end of the day, do perform your spiritual practices, but remember that you have to live in this materialistic world where there are different people living in different stages of Self-ignorance. Either you can become a complete recluse or you can act as a beacon sharing your knowledge and wisdom, but still, do so silently. Let your actions speak much more than your words. Never preach spirituality, people get offended too easily and quickly. When we try to describe the advantages of spirituality, there will always be some ignorant people who will get offended. But your interactions with the ignorant should never affect you, as a seeker. You now have the seeds of knowledge, let your knowledge grow into wisdom so that you can come out of any miseries with which your mind might seem to be controlling you. This will happen with the Grace of Self. You likely would have already noticed some subtle change in your consciousness as you have now reached the last page of this book and some of the knowledge will have translated into wisdom. I sincerely hope that you remain rooted in this Self of yours and yet keep your secret whilst interacting with others. A yogi should be able to remain resilient in the face of any adversity. As your wisdom grows you will feel much more strength in all difficult situations. Your Self will continue to guide you when you need it.

Ending Prayer

THANK YOU, O DIVINE, FOR GIVING ME THE OPPORTUNITY TO OPEN my body, mind, and intellect to the possibility of enlightenment. Thank you, O reader for reading this text, and I pray for you that you find your true nature. I wish to thank the Divine for the peace that this soul has gained by returning every material gain back to the source. I pledge that all the proceeds of this book will be used to further understand the scientific basis of spirituality through ongoing research on meditation and breathing techniques.

Printed in Canada